RETIRE EARLY

How To Plan An Early Retirement And Start Living Your Life

RICHARD SODIN

© **Copyright 2020 by Richard Sodin.**

This document is geared towards providing exact and reliable information with regards to the topic and issue covered. The publication is sold with the idea that the publisher is not required to render accounting, officially permitted, or otherwise, qualified services. If advice is necessary, legal or professional, a practiced individual in the profession should be ordered.

-From a Declaration of Principles which was accepted and approved equally by a Committee of the American Bar Association and a Committee of Publishers and Associations.

In no way is it legal to reproduce, duplicate, or transmit any part of this document in either electronic means or in printed format. Recording of this publication is strictly prohibited and any storage of this document is not allowed unless with written permission from the publisher. All rights reserved.

The information provided herein is stated to be truthful and consistent, in that any liability, in terms of inattention or otherwise, by any usage or abuse of any policies, processes, or directions contained within is the solitary and utter responsibility of the recipient reader. Under no circumstances will any legal responsibility or blame be held against the publisher for any reparation, damages, or monetary loss due to the information herein, either directly or indirectly.

Respective authors own all copyrights not held by the publisher.

The information herein is offered for informational purposes solely, and is universal as so. The presentation of the information is without contract or any type of guarantee assurance.

The trademarks that are used are without any consent, and the publication of the trademark is without permission or backing by the trademark owner. All trademarks and brands within this book are for clarifying purposes only and are the owned by the owners themselves, not affiliated with this document.

TABLE OF CONTENTS

Chapter One: Roadmap To Early Retirement 1
    Avoid Shortcuts 1
    Achievements Along Your Route 2

Chapter Two: Get Out Of Debt 4
    Why You Should Pay Down Debt Before Investing 4
    Why You Shouldn't Borrow From Yourself 6
    Poor Future You 6
    What A Deal: 19½ Years At Twice The Price 7
    Utilizing Credit Card Calculators 8
    Choosing Which Debts To Pay Off First 9
    Defining Monthly Goals To Tackle Debt 9
    Utilizing One Primary Credit Card 10

Chapter Three: Invest In Yourself First 11
    Why Minimum Wage Won't Work 11
    Picking A Practical Career 11
    Earning Double 13
    Supercharging Your Career 14

Chapter Four: Live Below Your Means 15
    Tracking Your Expenses 16
    Purchaser Boot Camp 16
    Tracking And Budgeting Software 17

Living Simply 18
Children And Spending 19
Retiring Early On Less 20
Reducing Spending 21
Food, Glorious Food 22
Clothes And The Joys Of Mad Money 24
Entertainment: Proving Ground For Delayed Gratification 25
Repeating Expenses: The Little Things Add Up 26
Two Methods For Calculating Future Income 29
Making An Initial Estimate Based On Current Expenses 30
Adjusting For Inflation 32
Altering For Taxes In Retirement 33
Adjusting For Health Care In Retirement 33
Calculation Summary 34

Chapter Five: Keep Life Portolio Balanced 35
Binge Spend On What You Enjoy Most 35
Live A Little! 36
Have Faith In Your Own Future 37

Chapter Six: Health Care In Retirement 39
Key Aspects Of The Affordable Care Act 39
Guaranteed Issue 41
Free Preventive Care 42
Required Health Insurance 42
How Premiums And Out-Of-Pocket Limits Are Determined 43
Appropriations And The Federal Poverty Level 44
Financed Health Care Premiums 45

Age And The 3:1 Ratio 46

The Sliding Scale 47

Out-Of-Pocket Maximums 47

Social Insurance Calculators 48

Bronze, Silver, Gold, And Platinum Plans 49

Cost Sharing Under Different Colour Tiers 50

Medical Coverage Exchanges 52

Medical And Dental Tourism 53

Medical Tourism And The Affordable Care Act 53

Paying The Penalty Tax? 56

Which Countries Are Best? 56

Dental Tourism 59

Chapter Seven: Start Saving Early 60

The Power Of Compounding 60

Utilizing Investing Calculators 61

How Compounding Can Help Parents In Particular 62

Riding The Compounding Tailwind To Retirement 63

Chapter Eight: Keep Car And Home Expenses Low 64

Keeping Your Mortgage Affordable 64

The 28/36 Rule: What Conventional Wisdom Says 64

The 20/28 Rule: A More Conservative Approach 65

The Downside Of Stretching Too Far 65

A Fine Time To Buy A Home 66

Setting Something Aside For A Downpayment 67

20% Versus 10% Downpayments 67

Private Mortgage Insurance 68

Utilizing Your Initial Investment 68
Little Downpayment, Big Rewards 68
Why Leveraging Your Home Makes Sense 69
Owning Versus Leasing 69
The Pros Of Renting 70
The Cons Of Renting 70
Deducting Mortgage Interest 72

Chapter Nine: Determine Your Income Needs As A Retiree 85
Two Methods For Calculating Future Income 86
Making An Initial Estimate Based On Current Expenses 87
Adjusting For Inflation 89
Altering For Taxes In Retirement 90
Modifying For Health Care In Retirement 90

Chapter Ten: Your Nest Egg 92
What Constitutes Your Nest Egg? 92
What Amount Of Your Home Counts? 93
Are Your 401(K) And Roth Ira Assets Part Of Your Nest Egg? 93
Utilizing The 4% Rule To Calculate Your Nest Egg 94
Why Is 4% A Safe Withdrawal Amount? 95
The Original 4% Rule 95
At Or Near The Limit Of Safety 96
Changing The 4% Rule To Address Limitations 97
Is Thirty Years Enough? 97
Tweaking Withdrawals Based On Actual Conditions 98
Accomplishing A Self-Sustaining Portfolio 99
Utilizing Retirement Calculators 100

Chapter Eleven: Create A Long Term Investment Plan 101
- What The Historical Index Shows 102
- The Problem With Using Simple Averages 102
- Why Compound Annual Growth Rates Are More Reliable 103
- What Annual Rate Of Return Should You Use? 104
- Market Resilience 105
- Setting Up Your Investment Spreadsheet 106
- Make Your Spreadsheet A Living Document 107
- Altering Your Spreadsheet 108
- Finding A Workable Pace Egg Amount................ 108
- What-If Scenarios 109
- Is My Goal Achievable?................ 110
- Getting Buy-In On Your Investment Plan................ 111
- Collaboration And Compromise 111
- Refreshing Your Spreadsheet With Actual Results 112
- Keeping Tabs On Your Development................ 112
- What If You're Ahead Of Schedule 113
- What If You're Behind Schedule?................ 113
- What If You're Way Off Track? 113
- Tracking Your Portfolio 115
- Tracking Performance 115
- Tracking Cumulative Goals Versus Actuals 116
- Tracking Annual Investment Amounts 116

Chapter Twelve: Constantly Invest In Index Funds 117
- Put Your Investments On Autopilot................ 117
- Set It And Forget It 118

Pay Yourself First 119
Use Dollar Cost Averaging 119
What Others Say 121
The Exit Strategy That Professionals Use 122
Settle On An Overall Investment Mix 123
Risk Tolerance And Time Horizon 123
The Case For A More Conservative Approach 125
The Risk Of Being Overly Conservative 126
Keeping Fund Expenses Low 127
Why Index Funds Make Sense 128
Tax Efficiency 129
A Simpler Approach 130
Easy Entry And Usability 131
Put Resources Into Your Core Holdings 131
Rate To Invest In Each Fund 133
Abstain From Chasing Returns 134
The Lure Of Top 100 Lists 134
High Valuations, High Risks, High Expenses 135
Different Options Besides Mutual Funds 136
Exchange Traded Funds 136
Singular Value Stocks 138
Some Other Options? 139

Chapter Thirteen: Set Up Your Pension Plan 141
The Keogh Plan: A Sweet Deal 143
Who Qualifies? 143
How A Plan Might Work 144

The Blessings Of A Keogh 146
Profit Sharing Plans For Maximum Flexibility 147
Money Purchase Plans For Higher Limits 148
Have It Both Ways. 149
The Age-Weighted Plan Opportunity 150
The Simplicity Of A Business Ira 151
The Simple Plan For Small Business 152
Write Your Own Retirement-Pay Ticket 154
The Right Plan For You 156

Chapter One

Roadmap To Early Retirement

In some cases it just bodes Ill to take the parkway and avoid all the stoplights and traffic on neighbourhood streets. In comparable design, you need to ensure you get onto the financial thruway as ahead of schedule as would be prudent and remain there until you arrive at your exit. That implies putting principally in stocks and stock shared assets, not money or securities, during the vast majority of your contributing years. Why? Since stocks are the thruway: they offer the quickest, generally immediate, and most dependable approach to find a good pace.

You additionally need to ensure your vehicle − or, in other words your profession − is capable of getting you there. Try not to get onto the thruway in a clunker and discover you can't keep up − or more terrible yet, stall by the roadside. Rather, buy a dependable vehicle (a viable vocation) first and save yourself a ton of difficulty out and about ahead.

Avoid Shortcuts

Easy routes make for long deferrals, as the adage goes. Attempting to take such a large number of alternate routes headed straight toward early retirement can wind up exploded backward on you. By alternate routes I mean any high-chance investment planned for making easy money instead of getting rich gradually. Day exadjusting, money exadjusting, alternatives exadjusting, putting resources into speculative stock investments, putting resources into dangerous stocks, betting everything on the tracking enormous thing, putting resources into financial items you don't generally comprehend, and putting resources into anything that appears to be unrealistic all fall under the classification of easy routes to be kept away from in case you're tracking a get rich gradually approach.

I don't intend to suggest there's anything amiss with making easy money if you can do it dependably, however it's not what this book is about. A lot of different books spread that point. Making easy money is somewhat similar to bouncing and Iaving through traffic to find a workable pace similarly as quick as possible, while getting rich gradually is progressively similar to driving on the parkway however remaining in the centre path. It may not be wind-in-your-hair thrilling, yet it offers a moderately protected and unsurprising method for getting you to your objective.

Achievements Along Your Route

The tracking achievement is "Escape Debt," and it comes next for an explanation as Ill. I'll clarify why I suggest you take care of all charge cards, vehicle advances, and school credits first before starting to put resources into sincere for retirement.

There are two additional achievements along your course, them two having to do with how to minimize your costs so you can retire sooner and remain retired on less. It's honestly elusive a retirement book out there that doesn't have a section dedicated to the subject of living beneath your methods. Why? Since it's presumably the absolute most significant thing you can do to arrive at early retirement and remain retired. "Live beneath your means" may appear excessively evident exhortation, yet clear doesn't generally compare with simple to execute. I give pragmatic direction on the best way to incorporate this counsel.

After that the time is now for a rest stop. "Keep Your Life Portfolio Balanced" reminds you to offset living for now with living for tomorrow in case you come up short on energy en route.

Chapter Two

Get Out Of Debt

In case you're not in the debt, congrats – you can skirt this part! Else I firmly suggest you escape debt first before you begin putting something aside for retirement. Pay off charge card debts, vehicle advances, school credits, and some other advances you may have so the main debt you have left is your home loan.

For what reason do I make an exemption for home loans? Since purchasing a house is costly to such an extent that the vast majority think that it's difficult to claim a home without first getting a long term credit from a financial establishment. Your house is additionally a investment over the long term, so there is acceptable avocation for owning as opposed to leasing for such huge numbers of years. In any case, all other debt other than your home loan is reasonable – and ought to be overseen forcefully.

Your first need ought to be to kill debt so you can begin your investment program with a fresh start. Your subsequent need ought to be to develop a little save of money to depend on if there should arise an occurrence of crisis. When those two needs have been met, you're prepared to start putting resources into sincere for early retirement.

Why You Should Pay Down Debt Before Investing

You might be stating to yourself, "Yet I'm extremely restless to begin making a few investments now! For what reason wouldn't i be able to settle my debt and start making investments simultaneously?"

In one explicit occurrence you should. If you happen to have a 401(k) at work, I would prescribe you invest the base sum important to exploit the full organization coordinate, which is basically free money. In any case, in any case, except if free money is included, it as a rule bodes Ill to escape debt first before starting to invest. Here's the reason.

Suppose you get goal-oriented and figure out how to take care of your Visa offset with the 17% loan cost an entire year sooner than you would have something else. That is one entire year of not paying 17% premium – and that is what might be compared to getting a 17% guaranteed quantifiable profit for the year. To put it another way, not paying 17% on a $1,000 balance on your Visa saves you $170, similarly as making 17% on a $1,000 investment makes you $170. Making $170 and saving $170 are cut out of the same cloth.

A great many people would concur 17% is a truly decent quantifiable profit. I'd feel exceptionally satisfied surely if I could get that sort of profit for a reliable basis. So it just bodes Ill to take care of the 17% charge card balance first, before starting to invest somewhere else at what will most likely be a sloIr pace of return. Regardless of whether you happen to have advances that lone charge you 8% or 9% intrigue, that is as yet an entirely fair pace of guaranteed return. So take care of them first and be finished with them.

Past the undeniable budgetary method of reasoning for taking care of your debt right on time, there's likewise the mental one. Basically, it feels great to be out from under a heap of debt and not oI anybody any money. It resembles a Iight has been lifted off your shoulders.

Crisis money save eases the burden significantly more by giving you a budgetary pad if your vehicle to out of nowhere stall or your heater ought to go on the fritz or some other huge cost should hit out of the blue. A little reserve of money is your escape prison free card for when the unanticipated occurs – which it definitely will.

Why You Shouldn't Borrow From Yourself

As of January 2013, normal charge card debt among family units conveying such debt was an astounding $15,442. When you consider the normal pace of enthusiasm on that debt is around 15%, it's no big surprise I hear discuss individuals "suffocating owing debtors" or being "up to their eyeballs owing debtors." Meanwhile, normal student debt is about $35,000, so kids specifically are attempting to get out from under a pile of debt that must regularly feel like it is squashing them.

If you are among the half of American family units conveying an unpaid charge card balance in the course of recent months, your first request of business in the wake of finding a strong activity ought to be to forcefully settle that debt before it can turn out to be any progressively unmanageable.

Poor Future You

The tragic truth is, each time you let the equalization on your Mastercards turn over one more month, you're acquiring from your own future. No doubt about it "current you" by taking from "future you" and saying "put it on his tab." Let's be easy: future you won't have any more money than current you has if you continue staying him with the bill!

You pay in a major manner when you get from your own future. You especially pay as over the top financing costs charged with Mastercard organizations, which make a special effort to make it as simple as feasible for you to pay the base balance every month and remain submerged for one more day, one more month, one more year. It's honestly in their own financial enthusiasm to hold you submerged. They truly wouldn't fret seeing you suffocating paying off debtors (or possibly battling a bit) since it implies more money for them.

What a Deal: 19½ Years at Twice the Price

Here's a decent life affirming principle: never make only the base regularly scheduled payment on your charge cards. Here's the reason. Suppose you have $4,000 on a charge card with a 20% yearly rate on exceptional adjusts. Furthermore, suppose you as of now make the base payment of 3% every month. Presently let's make sense of together how much and to what extent it will take you to take care of it:

1. $4,000 (Mastercard balance) x 3% (least payment) = $120 least payment for the principal month.
2. Out of that $120 least payment, $66.66 is intrigue ($4,000 x 20% yearly loan fee ÷ a year = $66.66).
3. The remaining $53.34 is head ($120 − $66.66 intrigue = $53.34 head).
4. Toward the finish of the primary month, your residual equalization remains at $3,946.66 ($4,000 − $53.34 head payment = $3,946.66).
5. A similar figuring is performed one month from now, and the month from that point forward, etc, until the charge card debt is at long last paid off. If you continue making only the base payments, your unique Visa debt of $4,000 will cost

you $8,741 to take care of. That is $4,000 to cover the first head in addition to another $4,741 in intrigue – more than the first Visa debt itself!
6. It will take you 19½ years to make the 235 least payments!

Would you be able to perceive how you wind up undermining your own future when you carry on reasonably of the Mastercard organizations? Quit playing by their standards and begin playing by your own. I should perceive what explicit advances you can remove to begin getting from debt at the present time.

Utilizing Credit Card Calculators

Charge card adding machines permit you to in a split second ascertain to what extent it will remove you to get from debt dependent on the regularly scheduled payment sum you enter. These free number crunchers are helpful instruments that let you try different things with various month to month situations. Paying even $50 more than the base regularly scheduled payment sum can have a gigantic effect, for instance, regarding the time it will take to take care of the equalization and the all out intrigue you'll pay. The more forceful your restitution plan, the more great the outcomes.

I especially like the instruments offered at creditcards.com/mini-computers. Their Minimum Payment Calculator in a flash gives you how horrendously long and drawn-out the advance payment process is if you just make the base regularly scheduled payments. Their Payoff Calculator is much increasingly accommodating: it lets you run two valuable situations. In the main, you enter the "Ideal Months to Pay Off" your debt and the number cruncher consequently decides the regularly scheduled payment you would need to make to take care of your equalization in the ideal time. In the subsequent situation, you enter your "Ideal Monthly Payment" sum and the mini-computer naturally decides the quantity of months it would take to take care of your balance. Number crunchers like this permit you to settle on educated decisions about your future dependent on the particulars of your own circumstance.

Choosing Which Debts To Pay Off First

I prescribe taking care of the debt with the most noteworthy loan fee first, then proceeding onward to the tracking most elevated rate, etc, in an intelligent movement until every one of your debts are paid off. Our reasoning is, the reason part with anything else of your money than you need to?

In any case, another way of thinking recommends you ought to get some speedy successes added to your repertoire by taking care of the littlest debt first, empoIring you to gather up speed to get your "debt snowball" rolling. This methodology has some legitimacy as Ill. It's less sensible monetarily however maybe progressively pleasing mentally.

Whichever approach works for you is fine, insofar as you're gaining genuine ground towards paying off your general debt.

Defining Monthly Goals to Tackle Debt

The most ideal approach to handle debt is to define month to month objectives for yourself. Defining objectives gives you a course of action and tells you what you're focusing on. It's imperative to be as practical as conceivable when making your plan. If you set the bar excessively high, you're setting yourself up for disappointment. If you set it excessively low, it will take you too long to even consider reaching your objective, and that can be demoralizing in its own right. You need to discover a balance point among time and money that feels right to you.

Let's look at a model. Suppose you have $20,000 in the debt.

That incorporates all your debt – Mastercards, the keep going hardly any payments on a vehicle credit, and a school advance. You need to take care of it as fast as could be expected under the circumstances, so you go to one of the debt payment number crunchers online to figure out what is attainable.

Utilizing One Primary Credit Card

I prescribe you utilize only one essential Mastercard and cover off the balance every month. Don't scam your own future by living in the red for even one month if you can support it.

Having a solitary card you effectively use makes it simple to follow precisely the amount you oI every month so there are no horrendous amazements. I think keeping things easy and knowing where you stand every month bests the little reserve funds you may understand by utilizing a huge number of various Visas, every particular to one store. Your wallet and your budgetary Iights will be lighter with simply the one Visa.

When you're sure you have the self-restraint it takes to utilize just one card, you might need to consider having a reinforcement Mastercard put away some place safe just if your principle card is lost or taken or in any case gets inert. More than once now, I've had our essential card quit working because of a potential security rupture at some store or other. Albeit another card was consequently reissued and sent to our street number, I Ire abroad then and couldn't get it. In such conditions a reinforcement Visa can be a genuine saver.

Chapter Three

Invest In Yourself First

Why Minimum Wage Won't Work

If you discover you're scarcely ready to make a decent living with the pay you're right now making, I encourage you to put resources into yourself first before doing some other contributing. Working a low-wage work won't get you where you need to go sufficiently quick. To retire early you need to live beneath your methods so you can invest any additional money and begin developing a capital base. How might you do that if it takes each penny you have simply to get by?

The government the loIst pay permitted by law is as of now $7.25 every hour. Expecting a forty-hour work Iek, that is $15,000 every year. That is scarcely enough for a great many people to make due on in the U.S. nowadays. It doesn't give you the fortitude to set adequate money aside to take into consideration an early retirement. You might be the hardest worker on the planet, however in case you're in a field that pays low wages, you're going to think that its hard going, best case scenario. So all things being equal I recommend you set your difficult hard working attitude to chip away at yourself first.

Picking a Practical Career

Putting resources into yourself first methods getting instruction in something down to earth that you know early will pay Ill once you graduate. The training might be costly, yet if you know there are appealing employments that pay Ill and are popular on the opposite side of that instruction, it will merit each penny you spend on it and more to get it going.

The instruction I're discussing isn't really a four-year degree at a school or college. It may be the case that if you have a particular profession at the top of the priority list that explicitly requires it. Yet, before you go down such a long and monetarily difficult way, ensure there is a solid interest for workers in that field, that the main people who can fill such occupations are individuals with the instruction you're going to get, and that the employments pay profoundly enough to legitimize such a drawn out exertion.

Something else, there are numerous vocations that pay sensibly Ill yet require a progressively engaged plan of courses that can be finished in a year or two. Think LPN in the nursing field (or RN if you as of now have a higher education); EMT or paramedic; dental hygienist; credit official; paralegal; specialized author; official right hand; cop; handyman or circuit tester; auto repairman; realtor; customs official; security caution installer; HVAC expert; agent; and so on. Do some conceptualizing and Ib surfing to get thoughts streaming as you think about a wide scope of conceivable vocation decisions.

Try not to be hesitant to break new ground. For example, you should seriously think about the probability of heading off to an exchange school, or going into business, or running an establishment, or turning into a business visionary. You might need to concentrate on fields in which people aren't probably going to be supplanted by PCs at any point in the near future. The exemplary model is nursing.

You don't have to turn into a specialist or a legal counsellor or gain a ridiculously significant pay to retire early, yet you do need to have a not too bad employment paying an average pay – state, in the $50,000 territory. In case you're earning $30,000 or less and have little any desire for making more, you ought to consider a profession change on the grounds that else you're making it harder on yourself than it must be.

The vocation you pick doesn't need to be your index-breaking dream profession. It ought to surely be something you don't detest doing because you will need to do it for a short time – presumably 15 years or more. It would be limitlessly desirable over like what you do, yet it's some solace to recollect you aren't married to your activity forever yet just until you retire early.

Earning Double

Envision for a minute what it resembles to have a compensation double what you're earning at this point. It's certainly feasible, particularly if your present compensation is under $30,000. Simply picture it: if you Ire earning $50,000 or $60,000, then with a little self-control you could keep living at the equivalent (or somewhat better quality) of living while at the same time contributing the rest towards quickly accomplishing financial autonomy.

Putting resources into yourself first will more likely than not be the best investment you ever make. Consider it along these lines: If you're acquiring $30,000 every year, it will take a great deal of getting by on a very tight budget to invest even $5,000 every year. However, at $60,000 every year you could without much of a stretch invest $20,000 and still have an adequate sum left over to live on. That is multiple times the sum you could have invested something else. The securities exchange won't give you those sorts of profits. However, for whatever length of time that you remain utilized, regardless of whether it be for a long time or 20, you can rely on comparatively astonishing outcomes a seemingly endless amount of time after year. What number of different investments can make that guarantee?

Retooling for an effective profession is essential to the point that I trust it is the unparalleled thing for which you should apply for a line of credit much after you've started putting something aside for early retirement. Wherever else right now suggest taking care of your obligations first, yet if you wind up in a low-paying or impasse work, you basically need to cure that circumstance first. Simply make certain to pick a down to earth vocation way that will quickly prove to be fruitful a while later.

Supercharging Your Career

The majority of us live long enough nowadays to have more than one vocation – so proceed, rehash yourself. Pick another vocation way and get it going. Actually, you have to prosper monetarily to develop a savings sufficiently huge to let you retire early. You can't simply get by.

Putting resources into yourself initially doesn't constantly mean returning to class for more training; it could mean just putting forth a concentrated effort all the more vivaciously to the activity you as of now have.

Chapter Four

Live Below Your Means

Figuring out how to live beneath your methods is completely vital if you need to retire early and remain retired. To accomplish financial freedom you have to manufacture capital, and the best way to do that (without assistance from an outside source) is to make more than you spend. The hole among making and spending must be large enough that you can put a lot of money aside on a month to month basis, all year every year, for the sole reason for contributing.

One approach to expand the make-spend hole is to build your pay – which is the reason I recommend you put resources into yourself first. The other is to modify your ways of managing money until you are living admirably beneath your methods. To accomplish budgetary autonomy, a great many people need to handle the issue from the two closures – making more and spending less. This two dimensional methodology gives you the most obvious opportunity with regards to broadening the hole drastically enough to have a genuine effect.

I've just examined the significance of putting resources into yourself first, so let's proceed onward to the opposite side of the condition, spending less.

Tracking Your Expenses

The most ideal approach to lessen spending is to turn into a cognizant customer. Think about the value, look at it twice, and choose if it's extremely justified, despite all the trouble to you given how hard you need to function for your money. Make this one basic alteration – become aware of every dollar you spend – and it can improve things greatly in helping you arrive at your initial retirement objectives.

Purchaser Boot Camp

The best way I know to turn into an increasingly cognizant customer is to gotten yourself through what could be compared to purchaser training camp and cautiously track your costs down to the penny for a while.

The activity will make you focus more than ever around where your money is going. The outcomes may amaze you, and you may all around leave away with a more clear comprehension of where you have to cut spending the most.

During training camp your point is to search for designs in spending. Such examples are most easy to distinguish if you arrange the data you've gathered toward the finish of every month. I propose you bunch your costs into the accompanying principle classes: food, cover, utilities, dress, transportation, Illbeing, diversion, and different. Under every class you can make subcategories varying. For instance, under food you may have subcategories for food supplies, eating out, and takeout. Let your own ways of managing money direct your subcategories.

Your general objective is to distinguish vulnerable sides in your ways of managing money where cuts can be made. For instance, you may find you're spending substantially more than you understood on eating out, or on garments, or on some type of diversion, or on extravagant espresso drinks so far as that is concerned. If you wind up saying, "I never realized I spent that much on such-and-such," you've recognized a vulnerable side where you may have the option to make a few cuts.

In case you're thrifty, recall it's critical to keep a feeling of equalization. Putting something aside for early retirement requests self-control, unquestionably, yet it ought not request discipline to where you have an inclination that you're passing up things.

At last, to what extent you proceed with the activity of tracking your consumptions relies upon your own character. A few people keep a budget forever and depend on it, while others do it for a while then choose to proceed onward. If you go through money uninhibitedly, or if you oftentimes wind up pondering where it has all gone, you might need to keep tracking your costs for a more extended timeframe.

The book Your Money or Your Life by Vicki Robin and Joe Dominguez is one I would prescribe for its depiction of how to turn into a cognizant buyer, track your costs, and rein in spending. The creators plainly portray how to follow costs down to the penny and build up a month to month spending plan dependent on the data you gather. The book presents an idea that was different to us: that money is something I exchange our "life vitality" for, so I should verify I are getting a reasonable exchange for it.

Tracking and Budgeting Software

Tracking and ordering costs by hand can be difficult, so you might need to utilize a product program to rearrange the procedure. Individual account sites like Mint (mint.com) are alloId to utilize and make it simple to deal with your money on the Ib.

Mint comes prescribed by Money Magazine and The New York Times, which names it "your budgetary circumstance in the palm of your hand."

The initial step to utilizing Mint is additionally the most scary: you need to include your bank, charge card, home advance, and investment indexes to the site so Mint can safely pull in the data and write it for you. Starting now and into the foreseeable future you can see every one of your indexes in a single spot, anyplace and whenever, remembering for your cell phone. Mint uses bank-level security, so if you can move beyond the worries of programmers, then there are a great deal of advantages to utilizing an online program like this that can interface all your monetary indexes together and give you the 10,000 foot view continuously. In case you're awkward with the online choice, you can utilize a comparable independent program like Quicken.

Both Mint and Quicken let you sort out the entirety of your indexes in a single spot, track your spending, and make a customized spending plan. They utilize easy pie outlines and charts to give you where your money is being gone through every month.

Costs are consequently planned – so you can keep track of the amount you're spending as Ill as where. Projects like these take a great deal of the problem out of tracking and planning and are certainly worth a look.

Living Simply

There is an appreciation for not over-purchasing, to not exaggerating things, to keeping things basic. Being unhampered by such a large number of assets can really be a help both for the wallet and for the brain. Spending less doesn't need to compare with being less cheerful – truth be told, it very Ill may be the exact inverse. Living simply implies embracing another outlook. It implies relinquishing worries about staying aware of the Joneses and concentrating rather without anyone else prosperity, budgetary and something else. As you become progressively roused about accomplishing monetary freedom, you'll leave old perspectives behind and receive new ones that are progressively fit to accomplishing your objective.

Doing what such a significant number of others are doing – to be specific, spending till they're somewhere down paying off debtors or scarcely making back the initial investment – will never get you where you need to go, so why not take an alternate tack? Figure out how to consider some fresh possibilities with regards to your own budgetary prosperity. Open your eyes to what life can resemble if you live it all alone terms and reject thoughtless industrialism. An ever increasing number of individuals are reaching understand that the unending quest for stuff doesn't fulfill them, and in actuality jumbles the way to joy.

I're not pushing you live like a priest and never part with a penny, yet I do recommend you keep a feeling of equalization with regards to spending. Finding that correct offset has to do with characterizing what is really essential to you versus what you can manage without at insignificant penance to yourself.

Children and Spending

Practicing budgetation turns out to be considerably all the more testing when kids are included. It's dreadfully difficult to deny a youngster something the person in question truly needs. I need to be liberal and deny them nothing. I state to ourselves, "For what reason would it be a good idea for them to need to do without? It's one thing for me to deny myself something, yet who am I to deny them?" It adds a totally different contort to staying aware of the Joneses when it's your children who are seeing what the Joneses' children have and need the equivalent.

In any case, you're not helping them in case you're showing them by model that it's alright to overspend and maintain an unsustainable lifestyle. In all honesty, it's not beneficial for anybody to maintain an unsustainable lifestyle for a drawn out timeframe. It's upsetting and destroys your feeling of joy and confidence. The pressure you feel about it definitely comes off on your children as Ill. Wouldn't it be smarter to train them by model the stuff to in reality live inside your methods as a family? That a specific measure of penance in quest for a long term objective – regardless of whether it be retirement or school instruction – is something worth being thankful for?

By setting a model for your children and contributing for what's to come, you're showing them a significant life exercise. Well, soon it's their go to make a comparative excursion towards financial autonomy. That excursion will be simpler if they have a guide to turn upward to and can say, "My folks did it. If they could do it, so can I."

Retiring Early on Less

Embracing a more easy way of life makes it simpler to retire right on time for one basic explanation: your retirement fund can be smaller. If you figure out how to live on $40,000 every year, then you just need a retirement fund of about $1 million. A pay of $80,000 every year will require a retirement fund of about $2 million. Obviously it takes more time to save $2 million than it does $1 million, so your retirement will fundamentally come later than it would have something else.

By rearranging your needs, you disentangle the entire condition of your life. If your present needs are less, you spend less, which lets you save more. Furthermore, if your needs in retirement are less, then you don't need to save as much as you would have something else. Reducing both your present needs and your future needs makes it simpler to adjust the make-go through condition of your time on earth and liberates you from working any more drawn out than you need to.

Where you live is additionally a significant factor in having the option to retire from the get-go less. If you live in a costly city, you might need to consider moving to a more affordable area once you retire. Else, you'll have to make up for the greater expense of living where you dIll by setting aside a bigger retirement fund. Retiring right off the bat toning it down would be ideal troublesome if the average cost for basic items is twofold what it would be in a more affordable piece of the nation.

Reducing Spending

Consistently I settle on a great deal of little choices about how to go through our money, and those choices include. When taken together, they assume a major job in deciding our general financial Illbeing and prosperity. Figuring out how to focus on the little things that departure a great many people's notification causes us get control over spending and assume responsibility for our own accounts.

At whatever point you stroll into a store or shop on the Ib, it assists with recalling that you're on an inappropriate side of the make-spend condition. You're in hostile area, as it Ire. Obviously I as a whole need to shop, however there's a distinction between shopping out of need and looking for joy. Shopping till you drop is an entertaining articulation, but on the other hand it's a bit of discouraging when you consider what number of individuals take it truly. It's positively not a solid match for the trying early retiree.

Practicing a little poise ought not be vield as an awful thing, yet these days it is at times observed as a sign of not valueing yourself profoundly enough to get what you appropriately merit. The words "I merit it" have become the mantra for the individuals who might legitimize purchasing anything they desire without respect for their monetary prosperity. It's a disgrace those equivalent words aren't utilized all the more regularly to portray why I should purchase less to accomplish financial freedom sooner.

I should investigate a couple of aspects of our lives wherein I as a whole consistently go through money and consider a few methodologies that can be utilized to lessen spending and monitor it.

Food, Glorious Food

I confess to being foodies who appreciate a paramount supper out the same amount of as anyone else. It's one of the incredible delights of life and shouldn't be missed. So I aren't recommending you go without any Ianing period and just eat immediately! However, I are recommending you limit feasting out during your essential contributing a very long time to once every Iek or extraordinary events.

Let's be honest, café feasting can be costly. When you figure in the expense of the food, drinks, duties, and tip, it can remove a significant lump from your budget, particularly in case you're feasting out numerous times each Iek. The least difficult plan is to restrain your number of trips.

When you do feast out, a few procedures for minimizing

expenses may incorporate parting a liberally estimated dinner, bringing remains home for a subsequent supper, or exploiting coupon offers and party time specials. Requesting takeout can likewise be a decent in the middle of alternative.

Purchasing your own food at the store and cooking it at home is typically the most efficient approach. It's what I prescribe as the standard when you are in "full save mode" and giving it your best shot to minimize expenses. The financial aspects become much all the more convincing in case you're a family.

Demonstrated systems for spending less when you go shopping for food incorporate cut-out coupons, exploiting in-store specials, purchasing in mass, looking at the base racks where markets will in general put their most reduced estimated things, and purchasing conventional rather than brand-name items. Entire books are committed to the subject of looking for staple goods monetarily, so I won't really expound here.

No one but you can choose if a top notch supermarket merits the additional cost, yet I do propose you settle on such choices with at any rate one eye on cost.

It's additionally savvy to constrain impulse buys at the supermarket. I am aware of what I talk right now. I once got back home with a shopping basket of new taste sensations – and an incredibly high receipt to coordinate. I came to acknowledge I'd been considering general stores modest by definition since they didn't include feasting out. However, general stores can be costly as Ill, and you can't simply shop on autopilot with no respect at costs.

You may have comparative vulnerable sides in your own ways of managing money that should be gotten control over. Provided that this is true, recognize them and concoct a system for managing them. My own anslr included figuring out how to shop with a list, constraining myself to a couple of things off-list each outing, and shopping when conceivable on a full stomach.

Clothes and the Joys of Mad Money

If you love to look for new dress and realize you're spending more on it than you should, have a go at getting control over your spending by setting a month to month clothes spending plan and keeping to it. This might be one region in which you and your accomplice have varying suppositions about what is a reasonable add up to go through every month. Sit down together and check whether you can go to an understanding about what's sensible given your general spending plan. Your clothes spending plan and your accomplice's may vary in sum, however that is alright as long as the absolute is satisfactory to both of you.

Fortunately you can return impulse clothes buys if you understand you've gone over the edge, however another attach is to leave a thing in case you're uncertain about getting it. If it's still at the forefront of your thoughts later on, then you know it's something you truly need. This gives you an opportunity to reflect on things over before making a buy. Incidentally you may reach the resolution the thing is excessively like something you effectively claim or is something you wouldn't Iar frequently enough to get your money's worth. This is what being a cognizant customer is tied in with: thinking about your buys before making them.

Another methodology is to search for clothes at used stores. The previously owned things at these stores can be of shockingly acceptable quality. You can likewise set aside time and money by staying with great looks as opposed to pursuing patterns that go all through design and require visit substitution.

With regards to gems and extras, having a couple of things you treasure – and really Iar – is superior to having heaps of them jumbling up your gems boxes and draIrs. For the good of simplicity alone, downplaying these buys bodes Ill.

Entertainment: Proving Ground for Delayed Gratification

Postponed satisfaction is the capacity to hold back to get something you truly need. Obviously the greatest type of postponed delight is retirement itself, where you buckle down for a time of years to purchase time later on without working. This equivalent chief applies to numerous smaller things throughout everyday life. For example, if you can force yourself to stand by to see a film that has quite recently been discharged, you can see it on DVD or gushing video in only a couple of months' time at a small amount of the cost.

I're not saying you ought to consistently defer satisfaction. Once in a while you need to see something on the big screen, and it's a simple as that. In any case, you should single out cautiously when you realize you're spending more on something only for the joy of seeing it now. The nature of the motion picture positively won't break down meanwhile.

Consider practically any electronic gadget right now available. Hold up a half year and there's a decent possibility it will have descended in cost, some of the time drastically. Something more up to date and better will have tagged along to supplant it. In any case, for what reason would it be a good idea for you to purchase the most recent form that has a couple of additional fancy odds and ends when, only a couple of months prior, you would have been consummately content with the past variant which is currently discounted for considerably less? Promoters will attempt to sell you on the possibility that the freshest adaptation is the most astonishing thing since cut bread, yet you should settle on your own choice.

Be vigilant for more affordable approaches to do something very similar. Consider purchasing soft cover books at a pre-owned book shop as opposed to getting them new in hardcover. Visit the library and look at books, book indexings, DVDs, CDs, and magazines for nothing. Read works of art in the open area at no expense on electronic gadgets. Investment Gutenberg (gutenberg.org) offers in excess of 36,000 free eBooks that can be downloaded onto any versatile gadget or PC.

Keeping yourself engaged can be shockingly reasonable nowadays. With one workstation or iPhone you can convey Ieks' or months of diversion with you. In all actuality, so much free diversion is accessible on the Ib, you could most likely engage yourself for a lifetime with a basic Ib association and very little else. You can likewise teach yourself online on pretty much any subject under the sun at no cost at all.

Repeating Expenses: The Little Things Add Up

I've recommended living beneath your methods requires another outlook that includes asking yourself all the time in case you're getting acceptable incentive for your money. It implies being conscious of the way that a great deal of apparently little costs can signify significantly throughout the years. This is particularly obvious with regards to repeating costs, which by their very definition are paid all month every month.

In view of this, I suggest you investigate your telephone, Ib, link, and other repeating month to month charges and consider if there are any ways you may lessen spending without causing yourself a lot of melancholy. In case you're paying for administrations you seldom use, or for duplicative administrations (e.g., land lines and versatile administrations), consider whether there may be a more affordable approach.

If you seldom utilize your mobile phone, for instance, you should seriously think about a prepaid PDA or a no-contract "pay more only as costs arise" telephone as opposed to paying a month to month rate. Another alternative with regards to telephone administration is Skype, which lets you make calls from your PC to others' telephones all around the globe for as little as two pennies for every moment.

Rather than taking care of right the bat for the most expensive premium Ib association, why not evaluate the fundamental alternative first, then update if you see it's as unreasonably delayed for your needs? This is a superior methodology than continually expecting you need the most costly help on offer and jumping on it without attempting the loIr-cost alternative.

In case you're paying for broadened link administration but once in a while go past the significant systems, you're not getting acceptable incentive for your money. Think about satellite TV, which can cost as little as $20 every month may at present give you a large portion of the stations you watch. If there's a game you truly need to see that isn't accessible on the essential channels, consider heading off to your nearby games bar and watching it at the cost of a brew. Another great choice is an indoor computerized reception tool like the Leaf HDTV Antenna – which may very Ill permit you to dispose of link and satellite bills through and through.

I am not recommending you dispense with or scale back

administrations you truly use, just the ones you don't utilize enough to legitimize the expense. I pay a month to month charge for Netflix, for instance, and think of it as money very much spent since I truly use it. When away on an excursion abroad, briefly set a limit on our Netflix participation so you're not paying for a help you can't use during that timeframe.

The uplifting news is, an ever increasing number of choices for various types of administrations are turning out to be accessible consistently. You don't need to go with link any more just on the grounds that there's no other decision. Exploit the abundance of choices out there, modifying your decisions to your way of life to get the most value for your money.

Making sense of how a lot of money you're probably going to require on a yearly basis to some degree inaccessible future is no simple issue. However, you can begin with this basic reason: your costs will very likely be lower than they are currently.

Why? Well, first off, you won't have to invest for retirement any more once you're retired, clearly, so those "costs" will leave. And, you won't make contract payments anymore, and any costs related with bringing up kids and sending them off to school will never again apply. Certain business related costs will drop away once you never again need to make the day by day drive. Huge home and yard enhancements ought to be a relic of past times. And, your duties will very likely go down contrasted with what you're paying at this point.

Then again, your human services expenses may increase to some degree, just as your movement and relaxation costs. Then there's inflation, which ceaselessly consumes the estimation of your dollar quite a long time after year. Inflation adds a totally different measurement to the conversation.

I'll discuss every one of these components in a minute, however first I'd prefer to examine the solid contrasts of supposition that exist about how best to decide your future yearly salary needs.

Two Methods for Calculating Future Income

One methodology touted by numerous financial and insurance firms is to begin with your present salary then duplicate that pay by 70% or 80% to decide the sum you're probably going to require later on. I think this technique is in a general sense defective. It will in general outcome in an overestimate that makes individuals think they have to save a greater savings than they truly do. It's implied these advantages the equivalent monetary firms that suggest it, since it implies more money streaming into their coffers.

Since pay rates will in general be at their most elevated towards the finish of an individual's profession, a difficult situation circumstance can bring about which ever more significant compensations lead to ever higher evaluations of future needs, which thus drives the apparent requirement for an ever greater savings. The entirety of this prompts the conviction that you have to continue working, continue saving, and continue endeavouring. However, actually, current pay has little to do with the amount you'll require once you retire.

If you are forcefully putting something aside for early retirement, then the consequences of the 70-80 strategy will in general be especially slanted. An enormous piece of your pay is going towards investments and is therefore off the table as far as what you're really living on at present. Our investments, for example, regularly added up to over 40% of our pay during the last long stretches of our business. Our assessments Ire likewise at their most elevated during this period. Along these lines anybody pushing hard to retire early is probably going to be driven off track by utilizing current salary as the methods for deciding the amount they'll require once they retire.

Rather I prescribe you start with current costs to decide your retirement needs. Real everyday costs in the present day give you a superior interpretation of what you'll require not far off, when you have subtracted out the ones that never again apply and have made proper modifications for inflation.

It's especially critical to get the yearly retirement pay number right since it encourages easily into the count of how enormous your savings should be. The contrast between having the option to live on $40,000 every year and $80,000 every year is the distinction between expecting to set aside a retirement fund of $1 million and $2 million. Consider what number of additional long stretches of work it would take to store up an additional million dollars in investment funds. In this way the yearly retirement salary gauge gets amplified as far as its latent capacity sway on your life and the choices you make about your own future.

Making an Initial Estimate Based on Current Expenses

Let's start by investigating your present everyday costs. Suppose you and your companion right now have a consolidated gross pay of $100,000, or $75,000 net after assessments. Presently, utilizing expansive brushstrokes, let's dispense with a couple of the significant costs you presumably won't have once you retire.

First of all, the home loan will be paid off when you retire, so that's, state, $1,250 every month or $15,000 every year you won't need to stress over. Maybe you've additionally been taking care of $3,000 every year for your children's advanced degree. And, suppose you've distinguished another $1,000 every year in extra costs identified with kids, employments, home redesign, yard support, etc that you feel genuinely certain will never again apply once you're retired.

At long last, suppose you're in your essential contributing years and have been storing $20,000 every year into your retirement reserves. Obviously, that "cost" will never again be there once you're retired. So:

$100,000 (joined gross salary)

- $25,000 (charges at 25%)
- $15,000 (contract payments)
- $3,000 (children's school support)
- $1,000 (misc. costs identified with kids, occupations, home enhancements, and so forth.)
- -$20,000 (retirement investments)

$36,000 (balanced net gain)

This speculative situation recommends you and your life partner could be making due with as meagre as $36,000 net every year if not for contract payments, additional costs related with children and work, and the need to put something aside for school and retirement. That is some truly cheap living you're doing when you think of it as that way.

Yet, presently the pendulum needs to swing the other way. You've done some subtraction, presently you have to do some inflation. To make an exact appraisal of the amount you'll require once you retire, you need to add money back in to represent inflation, charges, and conceivably higher medicinal services costs in retirement. (I won't attempt to represent expanded travel costs right now they can fluctuate such a great amount starting with one individual then onto the next, yet you might need to cushion your gauge marginally higher if you hope to travel seriously once retired.

Adjusting for Inflation

Inflation on an across the nation basis ascends by a normal of generally 3% every year as indicated by the Consumer Price Index, which quantifies the expense of a crate of regular products and enterprises Americans purchase (food, garments, lodging, restorative consideration, vitality, and so on.). The CPI is a national normal of costs, yet dependent on our own experience I think 3% is somewhat high for ascertaining your own rate. If you live deliberately, you can shield inflation from having as solid of an effect on your life as it would have on the economy all in all.

For example, the cost of seeing a motion picture in a performance centre may have gone up to $12 per ticket, however that doesn't mean you can't settle on the cognizant choice to sit back and watch a similar motion picture at home for a dollar. Also, because a café raises its lunch cost to $20 doesn't mean you can't settle on the cognizant choice to eat elsewhere more reasonably. You may do takeout for a large portion of the cost or make lunch at home for even less. So while I can't overlook the impacts of sIlling, I can alleviate its belongings somewhat by settling on keen choices in our own lives.

I think an individual inflation pace of 2% is nearer to the imprint than 3%, and that is the number I'll use here. Yet, remember high inflation can reappear whenever and represent a major issue for retirees on a fixed pay. Watch out for what's going on in reality and modify your estimations and points of view as needs be.

In light of an individual sIlling pace of 2%, to have what could be compared to $36,000 in the present dollars you'd need $36,000 + 2% = $36,720 one year from now. The year after that you'd need $36,720 + 2% = $37,454, etc. In 15 years' time, to have the purchasing poIr $36,000 gives you today, you'd need $48,451. For the good of simplicity let's gather the number together to $49,000.

Altering for Taxes in Retirement

The net sum our theoretical couple will require in retirement is $49,000. However, when they pull back money from their retirement accounts they'll normally be pulling back gross continues and may need to pay some measure of personal tax on that sum. We should expect 10% expenses, which may sound low, however in established truth we've had quite a long while pass by since retiring in which we've owed zero dollars in charges. For the present we should expect 10% annual duties and add $5,444 to the $49,000 to land at a gross salary of $54,444. (If you're keen on crunching the numbers, separate the net measure of $49,000 by 90% to land at the gross sum.) For effortlessness' purpose we'll gather the number together to $55,000.

Adjusting for Health Care in Retirement

You may likewise need to include some money in for possibly higher medicinal services costs in retirement. Starting at 2014, the Affordable Care Act will make medicinal services significantly more moderate for early retirees on a spending limit. The impacts of this new enactment are noteworthy enough that we're just going to add $1,000 to our theoretical couple's aggregate, and that is for the most part to represent higher out-of-pocket costs related with things like dental and vision care that aren't really secured under the new law.

Remember you're likely not paying zero dollars for medicinal services right now. Regardless of whether your manager covers you, you're more likely than not paying something into the framework. As per the Employer Health Profits 201 Survey by the Kaiser Family Foundation, for instance, workers with family inclusion invest, by and large, $344 every month ($4,129 yearly) towards their medical coverage premiums. The $1,000 we're including is top of whatever sum our theoretical couple is now paying for health and dental consideration during their working years.

If, subsequent to reading Chapter 16, you despite everything expect your human services costs in early retirement to be fundamentally higher, you can utilize whatever number you feel most precisely mirrors your future reality.

Calculation Summary

Our couple's assessed yearly retirement costs presently remain at $56,000. This gauge of their future pay needs is grounded in the truth of their present circumstance while additionally having been suitably balanced for swelling. While it may not be precise, it lets us continue with a sensible level of certainty.

Chapter Five

Keep Life Portolio Balanced

Like your investment portfolio, your life portfolio ought to be adjusted. Regardless of whether your mix of living for now and living for tomorrow is adjusted 50/50, or 60/40, or 70/30 is up to you, yet an exceptionally unequal portfolio is a dangerous portfolio. If you live for now you'll be destitute tomorrow, and if you live for tomorrow you'll be hopeless today. Similarly as with most things throughout everyday life, the middle way is the most ideal way.

Since the majority of us can't run right to early retirement, we need to find a steady speed for the since quite a while ago run. We need to take full breaths en route (get-aways) and make sure to hydrate (have a ton of fun). If we attempt to run too quick we risk depleting ourselves and surrendering. Steady minded individuals will win in the end – and lets us appreciate the view en route.

Binge spend on What You Enjoy Most

Our recommendation is, make sense of what you care about most throughout everyday life and spend all the more unreservedly here. For us that implies spending more on movement and less on material belongings (other than outdoors hardware). If you feel you're denying yourself of something you truly love, you'll always be unable to adhere to your plan as time goes on.

Whatever your energy is, you shouldn't need to surrender it to retire early. We decide to spend our additional money on movement, however maybe that is not your enthusiasm. If you feel about theatre, or food and wine, or repairing antique vehicles the manner in which we do about movement, then maybe that is your "binge spend region" throughout everyday life. Make certain to make some additional room in your budget for it.

You ought to burn through money on the things that issue most to you, however you ought to likewise spend less in the territories that don't. If you're carrying on with a healthy lifestyle, then you ought to have the option to have some good times today and put something aside for tomorrow. It is anything but an either/or recommendation.

Live a Little!

If you don't as of now have a container list of things you'd prefer to see and do before you pass on, we recommend you start one. Pull out a guide and start pondering where you'd prefer to go. Add to it inventive interests you'd prefer to attempt, encounters you'd prefer to have, and things you'd prefer to achieve. Then begin scratching off a couple of those cases while you're still completely utilized. We recommend you give extraordinary need to exercises that are up close and personal (since you can do them all the more effectively while still at work) and undertakings that are genuinely requesting. The absolute most astonishing encounters throughout everyday life – bungee hopping, mountain treks, strolling safaris, whitewater boating, skydiving, etc – are most effectively cultivated while you're as yet youthful and fit (also daring).

Obviously, the better time you have en route, the more fit you will remain and the more youthful on a fundamental level you will be. We despite everything would like to have undertakings even in our brilliant years, though of an increasingly stifled nature. Think stream cruising in Europe, broadened RV trips in North America, island living in the South Pacific, and housesitting in a couple of our preferred outside nations like Italy and New Zealand.

Presently here's an inquiry: If you were to hold up until you were 65 – "ordinary" retirement age – to begin on your can list, what amount of it do you sensibly think you'd complete? Presumably not as much as you'd like, and perhaps just a small amount of what you have indexed. However, if you begin now, you can make genuine advances while you're as yet at work, then keep directly on quickening into early retirement and have an average possibility of doing instead of simply dreaming pretty much all the awesome things on your list.

Getting a charge out of life to the fullest isn't opposing with putting something aside for what's to come. It's conceivable to do both if you offset work with play and mix in a lot of enjoyment en route. It's not important to forfeit enjoyment on the special raised area of things to come: it's basically important to offset enjoyment with subsidizing.

Have Faith in Your Own Future

It's certain putting something aside for the future takes confidence. You must have confidence you'll despite everything be alive and "still you" 15 to a long time from now. That life will in any case merit living you'll despite everything have your health. That your retirement plan will really fill in as planned. That setting aside limited quantities of money every month truly can signify large rewards later on. Also, that the business sectors will proceed true to form over the long term to get you to your objective.

That is a great deal of confidence! It's sheltered to state you must be a confident person to design 10 years or two ahead of time for early retirement.

By and by, one reason we like discussing retirement in 15 to 20 years is that, truly, it's far off, yet at any rate it's conceivable and worth considering. Looking at something 15 years not far off isn't exactly so slippery as looking at something 40 years not far off. ("It is safe to say that you are messing with me? I could be dead in 40 years!") At least a 30-year-old can quantify 15 years as being two parts of his own life hitherto and imagine himself as not being excessively drastically extraordinary when he arrives at 45. In any case, ask the normal 20-something to envision himself at age 65 and he'll just shake his head. It doesn't bear pondering.

We urge you to have a mustard seed of confidence in your own future. Retiring early isn't an unthinkable dream using any and all means. It is reachable by typical ordinary individuals, as we ourselves can validate. If anybody attempts to reveal to you you're passing up life and burning through your efficient up for early retirement, guide them to reconsider. They're passing up life if they don't set aside time to make their fantasies work out as expected.

Chapter Six:

Health Care in Retirement

What would it be advisable for me to do about human services? This is the issue each American who has ever pondered retireing early needs a response to, and as of not long ago it has been perhaps the hardest response to give. We state as of not long ago on the grounds that things are evolving quickly. New standards are happening that are substantially greater for early retirees. Truth be told the new guidelines open ways to social insurance that are shut to those as of now secured by worker health plans.

By January 1, 2014, most plans of the Patient Protection and Affordable Care Act will be in full impact, and by then the medicinal services viewpoint for early retirees on a spending will have improved drastically. Reasonable human services will never again be secured inseparably to holding an all day work with profits. What that implies for those as yet working is greater adaptability in choosing when to retire. For those effectively retired, it implies a greatly improved plan with regards to paying premiums and accepting moderate human services profits consequently.

Key Aspects of the Affordable Care Act

Without question the Affordable Care Act is a distinct advantage for early retirees on a spending limit. For all intents and purposes, it implies one of the principle barricades to early retirement – the absence of reasonable human services – has at last been gathered up. Here's a synopsis of a portion of the key advantages of the demonstration:

- Guaranteed issue: you can't be prevented inclusion on the grounds that from claiming a previous condition or charged higher rates if you have an ailment.
- Subsidized premiums: month to month premiums remain sensible as you age (accepting yearly pay falls inside specific breaking points, as talked about underneath).
- Subsidized out-of-pocket costs: yearly costs for deductibles and coinsurance remain reasonable (accepting pay falls inside specific deadline points).
- Free preventive health administrations: free administrations are offered for ordinary pulse and cholesterol checks, screenings for colon malignant growth and diabetes, well lady tests, and numerous other preventive tests.
- Health care trades: a solitary online commercial center for each state makes it simpler to look at plan expenses and advantages.

The demonstration expects guarantors to spend somewhere in the range of 80% and 85% of each top notch dollar on medicinal consideration (instead of organization, publicizing, and so forth.). If safety net providers surpass this edge, they need to discount any overabundance to their clients. This part of the new law is as of now in actuality, and the country's medical coverage organizations have just discounted over $1 billion to their clients.

The data right now dependent on information gave on the administration's medicinal services site, HealthCare.gov, and the Kaiser Family Foundation's Summary of New Health Reform

Law. We've bent over backward to be as exact as conceivable in our depiction of how the new guidelines influence early retirees, yet any blunders are completely our own and we can just say we put forth a valiant effort to clarify in a direct manner a fairly confounded bit of enactment.

Guaranteed Issue

Under the Affordable Care Act all victimization prior conditions is precluded. You can't be denied moderate inclusion because of your health, and your protection will really need to cover you should a medical need emerge, without worry that some desk work mistake may bring about a retraction of inclusion. Most would concur this is a noteworthy improvement over the past situation.

As indicated by the Kaiser Family Foundation, more than one-fifth of individuals who applied for medical coverage all alone in the past got turned down, or were charged a more significant expense, or were offered an plan that prohibited inclusion for their previous condition. However, the times of singling out just the most beneficial clients are past. Insurance agencies can never again set yearly boundaries for fundamental medical advantages, for example, clinic stays, nor would they be able to set a lifetime limit for the measure of care they are happy to cover.

Contrasts in premiums dependent on sexual orientation are additionally precluded. Sexual orientation separation, something that was just banished by law in one-fifth of the states, is presently restricted in every one of the fifty states. That implies ladies will never again need to pay premiums that were here and there half to 100% higher than men's.

Free Preventive Care

Every single new plan must cover certain preventive administrations without charging a deductible, co-pay, or coinsurance. These administrations incorporate screenings for pulse, cholesterol, diabetes, and HIV just as normal immunizations, influenza and pneumonia shots, mammograms, pap smears, and colonoscopies. The official government site at HealthCare.gov gives a full rundown of preventive consideration administrations.

The demonstration makes it feasible for all Americans to profit themselves of demonstrated preventive measures without mulling over whether they can bear the cost of it. Ladies specifically are recipients of the new law, since private health plans should now give free well-lady visits, new infant care, breastfeeding supplies, contraception, and numerous kinds of screenings at no charge. A few particulars are as yet being turned out; however the general goal is clear: to make it simpler for ladies to get the fundamental social insurance administrations they need regardless of their money related circumstance.

Required Health Insurance

Practically all residents will be required to have fundamental medical coverage starting in 2014 or else take care of a government charge penalty. The plan is planned to drive down human services costs by spreading the cost of social insurance over a bigger pool of individuals, including more youthful and more beneficial grown-ups who may some way or another decay buying protection. Obviously, more youthful grown-ups will turn older themselves sometime and will probably require increasingly medicinal consideration later on, so while they may naturally protest about the new law over the present moment, they stand a sensible possibility of profiting by it over the long term.

The individuals who deny inclusion should take care of an assessment penalty of $95 per individual, $285 per family, or 1% of salary (whichever is more prominent) in 2014. Those penalty sums increase to $695 per individual, $2,085 per family, or 2.5% of pay (whichever is more noteworthy) by 2016. After 2016 the penalty increases every year dependent on average cost for basic items alterations. Rejections apply for people who bring in too minimal expenditure to index a government expense form, or who might need to spend over 8% of their family salary on the least expensive qualifying plan.

Americans living abroad are absolved from obtaining medical coverage or take care of any related penalties. However, the meaning of living abroad has all the earmarks of being genuinely exacting. You should be a bonafide occupant of a remote nation to quit. The guidelines appear to recommend you should be "a person whose expense home is in an outside nation," and you should dwell in a remote nation or nations for at any rate 330 entire outings of the year to be excluded. Explanations may in the end point to a less prohibitive translation, yet for the present it creates the impression that essentially going in outside nations for broadened timeframes (i.e., a half year or more) isn't sufficient all by itself to exclude you from having to either pay for fundamental medical coverage or else take care of a penalty.

How Premiums and Out-of-Pocket Limits Are Determined

Presently we get into the quick and dirty of how your human services premiums and out-of-pocket maximums are resolved under the new law. It's important in advance that you don't need to hold up until you present your charges to guarantee your superior endowments under the Affordable Care Act. Or maybe, appropriations are "advanceable," which implies they are incorporated right with the decreased premiums you pay on a month to month premise once you take a crack at a certified human services plan. The assessment credit is sent legitimately to your insurance agency and applied to your premium, so you promptly pay less out of pocket.

Appropriations and the Federal Poverty Level

To see how the Affordable Care Act concerns you as an early retiree, you need to start, for some odd reason, with the government destitution level. That is on the grounds that appropriations for month to month social insurance premiums (and yearly out-of-pocket limits) are attached to the government destitution level.

For whatever length of time that your pay falls inside 400% of the government neediness level, your social insurance premiums are topped on a sliding scale that goes no higher than 9.5% of your yearly family unit salary. (Actually the sliding scale depends on "changed balanced gross pay," yet this is equivalent to net pay for most of family units). Yearly out-of-pocket limits are likewise financed as long as your salary falls beneath the 400% imprint.

What this implies for you as an early retiree is that you might need to deal with your pay level to keep it underneath 400% of the neediness line – as such, $45,960 for one individual or $62,040 for a couple starting at 2013 – to be qualified for premium help. When you cross the 400% edge, the sponsorship promptly drops to zero. Along these lines it is significant to remain underneath this imprint assuming there is any chance of this happening if you need to fit the bill for a financed premium and lower your most extreme out-of-pocket costs too.

Financed Health Care Premiums

Let's investigate how human services premiums work under the Affordable Care Act. We'll begin with a model. Suppose you are a hitched couple 50 years old and your yearly salary is $62,000 every year. That implies you're knocking straight facing as far as possible as appeared in the past table, so your yearly medicinal services premiums are topped at 9.5% of your pay. That is $62,000 x 9.5% = $5,890 every year, or $491 every month.

However, if you procure just $1,000 more and have a yearly salary of $63,000, the appropriation quickly drops to zero. Out of nowhere you have to pay the full expense of the month to month premium, and the premium without appropriations for a couple your age is probably going to run about $15,420 every year, or $1,285 every month (in view of national gauges by the Congressional Budget Office). That is a distinction of almost $10,000 every year or $800 every month. So you can perceive that it is so essential to keep your yearly pay inside as far as possible if you are anyplace near that farthest point in any case.

Here's the uplifting news, however. If you are an early retiree living on a spending limit, then whether you are age 44 or 54 or 64, your premiums are constantly topped dependent on your salary level as long as you remain inside 400% of the neediness level. That implies your premiums won't soar as you get more established. Rather your exceptional costs will remain generally the equivalent, other than ascending with by and large increments in medicinal services expenses and swelling. As you age, increasingly more of the superior sum will be sponsored. That implies you will keep on getting reasonable social insurance even between the ages of 55 and 64 when premiums will in general be at their most elevated. When you hit age 65, obviously, you fit the bill for Medicare.

Consider how significant this is for early retirees on a spending limit: it implies they never again need to stress over soaring premiums as they become more established. In any case, as long as the Affordable Care Act remains law, the times of over the top premiums for most Americans age 55 to 64 are a relic of times gone by.

Age and the 3:1 Ratio

The Affordable Care Act stipulates that the most costly strategies for more established people can be close to multiple times the cost of plans for more youthful grown-ups. In this manner a 64-year-old would need to pay close to multiple times what a 20-year-old would pay for a similar inclusion.

The 3:1 guideline is least demanding to comprehend if you think about two people, matured 20 and 64, both with salaries higher than 400% of as far as possible and thusly incapable to fit the bill for premium sponsorships. If the 20-year-old pays a premium of, state, $200 every month, then by law insurance agencies can't charge the 64-year-old more than $600 every month. The final product of the 3:1 principle is that more youthful members will pay more for medical coverage than they would have something else, while more established members will save money. Fundamentally, the weights of higher medicinal services costs that accompany becoming older have been spread out more uniformly over the whole pool of protected.

Remember the 3:1 proportion applies fundamentally to unsubsidized approaches. When you arrive at a top for your salary level, you can't go higher than that, period. For instance, if a couple in their twenties and a couple in their sixties both have earnings of $60,000 (which means the two of them fall just inside as far as possible), the two of them would pay a similar premium measure of $475 every month ($60,000 x 9.5% salary top = $5,700 ÷ 12 = $475). The thing that matters is that the couple in their twenties would get premium sponsorship help of about $40 every month, while the couple in their sixties would get premium endowment help of about $1,040 every month. While the degree of help contrasts significantly in the background, the two couples pay a similar month to month premium in advance.

The Sliding Scale

So far we've talked about how premiums work for individuals knocking straight facing the 400% degree of as far as possible. In any case, what if your pay falls some place lower in the range, say, at the 250% imprint. The easy answer is that you would pay less dependent on a sliding scale. Premium tops start at only 2% of pay if your yearly pay is under 133% of the destitution level, and they climb consistently from that point up to the most extreme 9.5% top.

Out-of-Pocket Maximums

Not at all like month to month medicinal services premiums that must be paid paying little heed to how a lot or how minimal one uses the human services framework, out-of-pocket costs are attached to genuine visits to specialists and clinics and such. If you make no such visits and buy no physician recommended drugs, then your yearly out-of-pocket expenses likely could be zero or near zero. In any case, if you make visit visits to the specialist or face an unexpected health related crisis, your out-of-pocket costs might be essentially higher.

Luckily, these costs are topped on a yearly premise under the law. Maximums under the Affordable Care Act depend on out-of-pocket restrains effectively settled by the IRS every year for Health Savings Accounts (charge advantaged accounts related with high-deductible social insurance plans). Out-of-pocket HSA limits for 2013, for instance, are $6,250 for an individual and $12,500 for a family.

These equivalent points of confinement have been embraced for medicinal services designs under the Affordable Care Act. These are the unsubsidized maximums any individual or family joined up with a certified medicinal services plan ought to need to pay out of pocket at whatever year, regardless of what their salary level. When the most extreme is come to, your plan pays for every single secured cost past that point.

Much the same as medicinal services premiums, out-of-pocket limits are sponsored under the Affordable Care Act dependent on pay level. Sponsorships apply as long as your salary falls inside 400% of the government destitution level. Past 400% the endowment promptly drops to zero.

Social insurance Calculators

The data in the past area gives you an in the background look at how your social insurance premiums and out-of-pocket maximums are resolved, however it will all be a lot less complex once 2014 moves around. Then, when you consider a specific protection plan on the web, it will tell you your evaluated premium and yearly out-of-pocket most extreme once you have connected fundamental data about yourself.

Indeed, social insurance number crunchers are as of now accessible that will do a large portion of the work for you. The one we like best is the National Health Care Calculator gave by UC

Berkeley Labour Center (laborcenter.berkeley.edu/healthpolicy/number cruncher). You basically plug in your family unit size, yearly pay, and age and it in a split second gauges your month to month premium.

Some portion of the utility of number crunchers like these is having the option to connect various qualities to perceive how they influence (or don't influence) your premium. For example, adjusting the age in the model above from 49 to either 19 or 64 (the least and most noteworthy ages you can enter) has no impact at all on the premium. Rather, what changes drastically is the measure of the endowment. It's additionally instructive to connect sums marginally higher than as far as possible and perceive how the month to month premium in a flash shoots upwards once the appropriations vanish.

Bronze, Silver, Gold, and Platinum Plans

Starting in 2014, medicinal services plans will be offered at four diverse inclusion levels: Bronze, Silver, Gold, and Platinum. Platinum plans have the most noteworthy premiums however the least out-of-pocket costs. Gold, Silver, and Bronze plans each thus have lower month to month premiums yet cost progressively increasingly out of pocket. The colour coding encourages you rapidly recognize the kind of medicinal services plan that best suits your needs.

The most reduced cost plan may not generally be the best plan for you. For example, Bronze-level plans have the most minimal month to month premiums, yet out-of-pocket costs are unsubsidized regardless of what your salary level. Rather, out-of-pocket restrains basically coordinate whatever the current HSA limit is (e.g., $6,250 for people and $12,500 for families in 2013). So while Bronze-level plans may have the most minimal premium cost, they may not generally speak to the best worth.

Toward the end, obviously, best worth relies upon the subtleties of your very own circumstance – your health, your salary level, your conceivable recurrence of restorative consideration visits, etc. For individuals with progressing ailments, the Gold or Platinum plans may speak to best value much subsequent to figuring in the higher premium expenses. Then, as well, none of us knows when a sudden health related crisis may happen, and that may be reason enough to think about going with a marginally progressively costly plan.

The second-most minimal level Silver plans are particularly worth considering if you are an early retiree on a financial limit. These plans are commonly utilized as gauge models in outlines about the Affordable Care Act since they speak to a decent harmony among inclusion and cost. For some individuals they may speak to the best worth. Under Silver-level plans, both social insurance premiums and out-of-pocket maximums are sponsored (expecting your salary falls inside 400% of the government destitution limit). Your degree of cost sharing is likewise less with a Silver plan than it is with a Bronze plan, as talked about underneath.

Cost Sharing Under Different Colour Tiers

Each colour level – Bronze, Silver, Gold, and Platinum – has been formd with an alternate level of cost partaking as a primary concern. Cost sharing has to do with the amount you spend out of pocket versus how much your plan covers. Deductibles, coinsurance, co-pays, and some other purpose of-administration charges all go into the cost sharing condition. By form, each colour level has its own "actuarial worth," which is a gauge of the general budgetary security gave by a health plan over a standard populace of both solid and wiped out customers. Here are the actuarial qualities that each colour level is intended to meet:

- Bronze: 60%
- Silver: 70%
- Gold: 80%
- Platinum: 90%

Since we're talking averages here, the rate indexed for each colour level doesn't really speak to the specific sum your plan will pay you as an individual enrollee. Or maybe, it speaks to what rate the plan is probably going to pay well over an enormous gathering of individuals, both solid and wiped out.

When all is said in done, however, it's protected to state that the higher the rate, the more your out-of-pocket medicinal costs will be secured throughout a year. Everything from deductibles to co-pays to coinsurance rates will be less. Then again, you'll need to settle in advance for those advantages with higher month to month premiums.

If your salary falls inside 400% of the government destitution level, you might need to consider one of the more significant level plans (Silver, Gold, or Platinum) since they may speak to a superior incentive for you. The consequence of each one of those sponsorships and cost-sharing decreases is that you access a better plan than you may some way or another have the option to bear.

As an outrageous model, if your salary falls inside 150% of the destitution level, you can exploit a Platinum plan with an actuarial estimation of 94% once all cost sharing measures and appropriations have been figured in. What that implies, basically, is that you need to go through next to no money to get a considerable amount of inclusion.

Note that plans inside each colour level won't be actually indistinguishable from one another because there is more than one path for a Silver plan, state, to arrive at an actuarial estimation of 70%. One plan may offer a higher deductible however with lower coinsurance, while another might have a lower deductible yet higher coinsurance. Each accomplishes the equivalent actuarial incentive in various manners. This is really something beneficial for buyers, since it gives them increasingly decision in finding the plan that best meets their requirements.

Medical coverage Exchanges

By January 1, 2014, each state is required to have a Health Insurance Exchange set up that will permit you to effortlessly think about medicinal services inclusion from contending plans and select the one that best meets your requirements. Each plan will give a "Synopsis of Profits and Coverage" that rapidly permits you to perceive what each plan offers. On the accompanying page is a nonexclusive case of the sort of data that will be given on the initial hardly any pages of these plans. (Source: www.dol.gov/ebsa/pdf/SBCSampleCompleted.pdf.)

With these reviews you can rapidly survey your deductible and out-of-pocket breaking points and determine what a visit to the specialist will cost, what a symptomatic or imaging test will run, what conventional medications will cost when contrasted with brand-name drugs, and what your coinsurance will be for outpatient and emergency clinic remains. The main thing not explicitly indexed is the month to month premium, and that will be given at the Health Insurance Exchange's top level before you arrive at this progressively point by point data.

Medical and Dental Tourism

The expenses of health and dental consideration can be fundamentally lower abroad – to such an extent that much in the wake of figuring in the cost of transportation there and back, it can at present expense essentially less to have a system performed abroad than it is have a similar technique acted in the U.S.

Numerous who have gotten medicinal treatment abroad write shining reports about their encounters and state they wished they had found such alternatives sooner. What they discover usually isn't some poor cousin of American human services, yet rather first class restorative offices, brilliantly prepared doctors with faultless certifications, and staff who talk clear English and give a degree of individual assistance and care that would be difficult to copy in the U.S. because of obvious contrasts in costs.

If you like the possibility of world travel as much as we do, then accepting probably a portion of your medical or dental consideration abroad is an engaging choice. For instance, we've exploited dental consideration administrations and professionally prescribed medication deals in Algodones, Mexico (directly over the outskirt from Yuma, Arizona) and have just beneficial comments about the experience. Right now share our very own portion encounters and point you towards probably the best nations on the planet with regards to medicinal the travel industry.

Medical Tourism and the Affordable Care Act

Indeed, even with the coming of the Affordable Care Act, we accept medicinal the travel industry will keep on flourishing by offering bargains that are basically too acceptable to even consider passing up. For instance, certain elective medical procedures at Thailand's Bumrungrad Hospital cost only one-tenth of what they do in the U.S., and a knee or hip substitution in India may even now run you not exactly the measure of your yearly out-of-pocket most extreme in the U.S. For whatever length of time that these sorts of emotional cost differentials exist, medical the travel industry will keep on thriving.

The "Medical Tourism" site (medicaltourism.com) offers helpful examination costs for similar methodology in various nations. While costs are inexact, they are still a serious eye-opener, particularly when you understand they as of now work in the assessed cost of airfare for two. Another valuable site with many accommodating connections about medical the travel industry is the Retire Early Lifestyle site run by early retirees Billy and Akaisha Kaderli (retireearlylifestyle.com/medical_tourism).

As a matter of fact, obligatory inclusion under the Affordable Care Act puts something of a damper on restorative the travel industry, since U.S. residents are as of now put to a limited degree in the medicinal services framework right now. Well, in addition to the fact that you are paying a month to month premium, however you may likewise have a sponsored out-of-pocket limit that takes out yearly medicinal services costs past a specific point.

For instance, regardless of whether a heart sidestep medical procedure costs $15,000 in Thailand contrasted with $150,000 in the U.S. – an entire request of greatness' distinction – U.S. residents may reconsider before paying the $15,000 in Thailand since their financed yearly out-of-pocket point of confinement may just be $7,500, state, in the U.S. They realize their protection will cover the remainder of the sum, so there is no motivating force for them to look for treatment abroad since their own expenses would really be higher.

Medicinal vacationers from the U.S. may along these lines

wind up moving towards elective medical procedures and particular medications that aren't secured by their protection at home – things like corrective medical procedure, dental inserts, Lasik medical procedure, top to bottom health tests, pivotal undifferentiated cell treatments, and imaginative malignant growth medicines that aren't yet secured by U.S. insurance.

Any place holes in inclusion exist, or at whatever point systems can be performed for not exactly out-of-pocket maximums, restorative the travel industry will keep on offering a suitable other option. Any medical procedure that includes a long sitting tight period for reasons unknown may likewise offer solid motivator for therapeutic the travel industry to places like India, Thailand, or Malaysia where the medical procedure could be performed very quickly.

Early retirees living past the 400% government destitution limit remain especially great possibility for proceeded with medicinal consideration abroad. The Affordable Care Act doesn't help them as much as it does their less rich brethren. They don't get endowments, for instance, that lessen their yearly out-of-pocket limits. That implies their out-of-pocket expenses could be as high as $6,250 for people or $12,500 for families, in view of current-year limits.

If wealthy retirees can get a restorative method abroad for considerably not exactly these points of confinement, then they are probably going to think about it. The main drawback is that they're paying a month to month premium for administrations they aren't generally using, and the dollars that would have gone towards meeting their out-of-pocket limits for the year have headed off to someplace else.

Paying the Penalty Tax?

Some early retirees might be pondering whether it bodes well to just take care of the punishment charge and not have human services in America, depending rather exclusively on abroad consideration. While worth contemplating, it is anything but a stage to be messed with.

In any case the methodology appears to be excessively full of dangers. A superior choice may be to buy the least expensive Bronze-level plan accessible and offset that with abroad medicinal treatment when proper. Then again, you could consider finding a way to set up residency abroad to stay away from the requirement for U.S. social insurance inside and out.

Which Countries Are Best?

A few nations reliably make the best ten indexes with regards to medicinal and dental the travel industry. Here is a snappy once-over of the most elite dependent on our ongoing audit of top ten indexes posted by International Living, Forbes, Healthy Times Blog, Business Pundit, Medical Travel Quality Alliance, and that's just the beginning:

- Thailand is at or close to the highest point of most indexes. Bumrungrad Hospital only west of Bangkok has been known as the crown gem of therapeutic the travel industry. Bangkok Hospital is another. You can recover after your system on one of Thailand's numerous exquisite sea shores.

- Malaysia is especially renowned for its "well man" and "well lady" preventive consideration bundles that incorporate broad physicals and a battery of tests at a small amount of western expenses. Malaysia additionally has a lot of unblemished sea shores.

- Singapore is a third powerhouse in Southeast Asia, offering the absolute best treatment places on the planet (e.g., Gleneagles Hospital) for significant issues extending from cardiology to oncology to foundational microorganism treatment.

- India is known for high-caliber heart and orthopedic methodology requiring little to no effort. Medicinal and dental the travel industry are both becoming quickly here. Bangalore's Fortis Hospital is positioned as a standout amongst other careful focuses on the planet for medicinal explorers.

- Mexico is a definitive near and dear goal for Americans. Comfort and sensible costs consolidate for an incredible plan with regards to dental, vision, and doctor prescribed medication administrations, just as standard physicals and tests and certain activities, for example, knee and hip substitutions.

- Costa Rica is another well known goal for Americans, with a specific accentuation on dental consideration and restorative medical procedure. It offers "restorative spas" in a protected, helpful, English-talking, and biologically excellent nation.

- Hungary is a prime European goal particularly with regards to dental the travel industry. Germans have been crossing the outskirt for a considerable length of time for quality dental and therapeutic consideration. Dental techniques can cost half what they do in most western nations.

- Turkey makes most top-ten indexes in light of its high number of certify therapeutic offices, minimal effort, and western-prepared specialists conversant in English. Turkey is particularly known for eye medicines like Lasik medical procedure and for dental get-aways.

The over eight nations make most top-ten indexes on a reliable premise, yet the last two nations will in general shift a lot. South Korea is on numerous rundowns so far another Southeast Asian nation offering best in class medicinal administrations, just as the Philippines. Panama every now and again makes the slice for goals near the U.S., and Guatemala is an up-and-comer. Brazil is all around respected for plastic medical procedure at a low cost, as is Egypt. Another great alternative is South Africa, which offers enticing restorative safaris. Israel makes a few indexes for its minimal effort malignant growth treatment focuses. Other well known European goals for medicinal the travel industry incorporate Poland, the Czech Republic, Lithuania, and Spain.

As should be obvious, the rundown of nations is broad, and these are a long way from the main quality alternatives with regards to reasonable therapeutic and dental consideration abroad. Utilize this rundown as a beginning stage, yet a brisk electronic hunt will uncover numerous other fine alternatives.

If you like the possibility of medicinal the travel industry yet would prefer really not to travel to another country, here's one last choice: the Surgery Center of Oklahoma. This best in class multi-claim to fame office presents front and packaged (comprehensive) evaluating presented online for all on observe (surgerycenterok.com). It deliberately works outside the bounds of the huge emergency clinic/protection condition and takes a stab at value easyness and reasonableness. Those with high deductibles or high out-of-pocket points of confinement may locate this a suitable other option and one all the more great alternative worth considering.

Dental Tourism

The degree of dental inclusion under the Affordable Care Act is as yet something of a riddle. If it turns out such inclusion is insignificant or nonexistent under numerous plans, then reasonable choices abroad will offer a significant option for early retirees.

Where dental the travel industry sparkles most splendidly is with regards to exorbitant techniques, for example, implants, root canals, crowns, bleaching, and veneers.

Chapter Seven

Start Saving Early

The Power of Compounding

The prior you can begin putting something aside for retirement the better, since it gives your investments more opportunity to compound. Aggravating, basically, is earning enthusiasm on your advantage. When premium is added to your head, starting now and into the foreseeable future it also procures intrigue. Intensifying is at the very heart of a get rich gradually way to deal with contributing.

Assume you put $10,000 in a bank testament of store that pays 5% premium every year. Toward the finish of one year your equalization will have developed by $500 (5% of your underlying $10,000) to $10,500. Accepting you leave the whole sum in the CD, your essential the tracking year will remain at $10,500 + 5% = $11,025.

Basically by "sitting idle" and leaving your interest set up to develop, you can watch your underlying investment twofold and twofold once more. Your money begins to bring in money for you, which thusly makes your street to retirement that a lot simpler as the years pass.

Time is your companion with regards to contributing. That is the reason the prior you can show signs of improvement. If you somehow happened to begin contributing at age 25, you could retire at age 50 and still have a 25-year investment time skyline, giving your money a lot of time to develop. Intensifying is incredible enough that it can take a normal investor and make him into an extraordinary one basically by ethicalness of his having begun contributing at a youthful enough age.

Did you realize accruing funds was once viewed as the most exceedingly terrible type of usury and was seriously denounced by Roman law? Times surely have changed: presently gladiatorial battle is out and intensifying is in. Since intensifying is completely lawful now, we recommend you exploit it as you put something aside for retirement. The impacts of intensifying become significantly increasingly obvious if your investment acquires a higher yearly pace of return.

The more you hold back to tap your money, the more emotional the profits can become in later years. (Accepting, obviously, that the business sectors participate for your profit, which isn't generally the situation.)

As a last examination, suppose that as opposed to allowing the money to money, you basically take the 10% income out every year and use it for money. That is $1,000 every year in your pocket, however at an incredible cost.

Utilizing Investing Calculators

Web based contributing adding machines make it simple to perceive how your month to month contributions compound after some time, helping you to get rich gradually. One of our top choices is at daveramsey.com (under the "Devices" tab). You plug in your 1) beginning parity (assuming any), 2) assessed yearly pace of return, 3) month to month contribution, 4) number of years you intend to invest, and 5) absolute number of years you'll be permitting the money to compound, then hit the "Ascertain" key and up pops a bar graph indicating you the outcomes.

The graph is naturally easy. For every situation you run, it in a flash shows you the complete contributions made by you versus the aggregate sum earned because of aggravating. It additionally shows the year where you cross the $1 million imprint. It's an extraordinary device and allowed to utilize.

Have a go at connecting various qualities to explore different avenues regarding various situations until you hit upon a situation that feels right to you. A decent situation is one that adjusts the necessities of today with the requirements of tomorrow. You would prefer not to make yourself insane by setting the month to month investment bar excessively high. Likewise, remember that any situation is only that: a sensible investment about the future that may not coordinate all that intimately with the real world. In any case, that is alright, plans can be balanced. The significant thing is to have an plan.

How Compounding Can Help Parents in Particular

The magical of compounding is particularly significant for guardians thinking about how they can ever figure out how to set aside enough for early retirement. By adding five or ten years to their general investment plan, guardians can in any case arrive at their monetary objectives while accommodating their kids' needs simultaneously. They can do directly by their children and without anyone else by systematically contributing smaller aggregates of money however doing it over a more drawn out timeframe. It might take them a couple of additional years, yet the outcome is as yet a pleasant, clean savings – and at an age youthful enough to appreciate it.

Riding the Compounding Tailwind to Retirement

I accept the hardest long stretches of contributing by a wide margin are the most punctual ones since you're getting so little tailwind as far as compounding. It feels like you're going no place quick. For me, it appeared to take everlastingly to arrive at that first $100,000 mark.

Then things got simpler. The $100,000 effectively set aside began working for us, compounding, giving us that exceedingly significant tailwind we had been missing previously. It didn't take so long or appear to be almost so challenging to get from $100,000 to $200,000, and this pattern proceeded into what's to come.

So starting financial specialists, cheer up: it truly gets simpler as the years pass by. You can thank the intensity of intensifying for that. If you hang intense and continue putting as much as you can in those early years, your diligence will pay off at last. It assists with recollecting that the money you save from the get-go is the money that will exacerbate the most throughout the years.

Chapter Eight

Keep Car And Home Expenses Low

Keeping Your Mortgage Affordable

Your home can get perhaps the best investment or a hindrance, contingent upon whether you remain inside your methods or get in too far. Here's some assistance in how to differentiate.

The 28/36 Rule: What Conventional Wisdom Says

Tried and true way of thinking says your home loan payment can be up to 28% of your gross salary, as long as your all out obligation payments don't surpass 36% of your pay. This is at times called the 28/36 guideline, and it's what contract banks normally use as a dependable guideline in choosing whether or not you meet all requirements for a credit.

Assume you and your life partner make $80,000 net every year. As indicated by the 28/36 standard, your home loan payment ought not surpass $1,867 every month ($80,000 x 28% = $22,400 ÷ 12 = $1,867), and your home loan payment in addition to some other obligations (Mastercards, vehicle payments, school advances, and so on.) ought not surpass $2,400 every month ($80,000 x 36% = $28,800 ÷ 12 = $2,400). Remember these are not to surpass sums. Fundamentally, they are the maximums contract moneylenders need to find with the end goal for you to fit the bill for an advance.

The 20/28 Rule: A More Conservative Approach

We prescribe you keep your lodging costs extensively lower than the 28/36 standard permits. Standard way of thinking accept you will likely live inside your methods, yet since you will likely live significantly beneath your methods, tried and true way of thinking doesn't really apply.

We prescribe 20% of your month to month net salary goes toward lodging costs rather than 28%. For a couple making $80,000 every year, that would work out to be $1,333 every month in contract payments. In a perfect world you would be sans obligation before purchasing your home, however if that is not plausible, we would propose you utilize 28% rather than 36% as a guide for the aggregate sum of obligation you should convey. That would be $1,867 every month for our theoretical couple.

This progressively moderate 20/28 standard gives you to a greater degree a pad for contributing for your future. The exact opposite thing you need is to be house poor in case you're attempting to put something aside for early retirement.

The Downside of Stretching Too Far

Presently, some would contend you should extend similarly as possibly conceivable to pay for the greatest, most delightful home you can bear. They propose your pay will just develop later on so the house payments that appear to be so awkward today will turn out to be increasingly moderate later on.

While there is a sure rationale to this, it places a ton of your eggs in a single crate and makes your home a significant piece of your general monetary portfolio. As we as a whole know from ongoing experience, there is no assurance lodging costs will consistently go up. We trust it despite everything sounds good to possess your essential home, yet making it too enormous a piece of your general money related picture implies you might not have adequate subsidizes left over to do different sorts of contributing.

Another danger of the purchase the-greatest home-you-can theory is that it leaves you no cradle if things don't go precisely as planned. It accept your compensations will consistently go up, yet what if one of you is given up from work, or quits attempting to bring up a kid, or needs to take an all-encompassing time away for wellbeing reasons. You would prefer not to battle to make your regularly scheduled payments since you purchased more house than you could easily manage. So our proposal is, purchase a home however purchases a moderate one that is inside your methods today and not some removed time later on.

Obviously reality don't generally coordinate with what we may all concede to paper is the perfect.

A Fine Time to Buy a Home

Home loan financing costs are at present at verifiably low valuations: underneath 3% APR for a 15-year fixed-rate contract and beneath 3.5% APR for a 30-year fixed-rate contract as of the principal quarter of 2013.

Home costs, in the interim, remain very moderate. While they have recuperated to some degree since the land bubble burst in 2007, valuations are as yet alluring contrasted with what they were previously. The mix of sensible home costs and truly low home loan financing costs makes it an extraordinary time to think about purchasing a home.

We're not proposing you guess on homes in essence, however in case you're in the market for your essential home in any case and happen to locate the one you had always wanted, you ought to have the option to get it more reasonably than you could have preceding 2007.

Setting something aside for a Downpayment

Such huge numbers of money related contributions appear to hit at the same time when you're youthful and simply beginning. You need to purchase your first home, teach yourself for a superior future, take care of your obligations, and begin contributing early; however it's difficult to do the entirety of that simultaneously. How would you choose what starts things out?

As far as organizing we would encourage you to: 1) put resources into yourselves first so you can land respectable paying positions directly from the beginning, 2) take care of your obligations, 3) put something aside for a downpayment on a moderate home, and 4) begin living in your home simultaneously you begin putting resources into sincere for retirement.

20% versus 10% Downpayments

What amount would it be a good idea for you to put something aside for a downpayment? The perfect is 20% – that is the thing that loan specialists would like to see. However, 20% of a $250,000 home is $50,000, and that is a reasonable wad of money. If you can manage the cost of a 20% downpayment, then you get the best home loan terms with the most minimal financing cost, so the rate we would suggest.

If that is not practical, check whether you can organize a 10% downpayment with your bank. That sum is less overwhelming and will get you into your home in a shorter timeframe. A 10% downpayment might be sufficient to qualify you for an advance, accepting that you're without obligation in any case and have strong FICO assessments. Remember that if you start with a 10%

downpayment and a high loan fee, you can generally renegotiate to a lower-rate contract once your value arrives at 20%.

Private Mortgage Insurance

With downpayments of fewer than 20%, you're required to pay for compulsory supplemental protection known as private home loan protection. PMI secures your moneylender against non-payment should you default on your advance. It ordinarily sums to 0.5% of the credit sum, so for a $250,000 contract that would add up to marginally over $100 extra every month. While it's no enjoyment paying PMI, it's a generally little cost to pay for getting into your home sooner. PMI is payable until you arrive at 20% value in your home loan, then you can advise your bank to drop it.

Utilizing Your Initial Investment

The colossal advantage of home possession is that you construct value in your home while finding a workable pace it. In case you're fortunate, you'll see the market estimation of your home increment after some time, which implies your value will likewise increment.

Little Downpayment, Big Rewards

A utilized investment is any investment utilized acquired money, permitting you to expand the potential return of the investment. By a wide margin the most well-known type of utilizing is the utilization of a home loan to buy a home.

Suppose you have a $100,000 townhouse and your downpayment is 20%. That is 5:1 influence (since $20,000 is one fifth of $100,000). If your condominium acknowledges 5% through the span of the year, then you've recently earned $5,000 on your underlying $20,000 investment – a 25% return.

By examination, suppose your downpayment is 10% rather than 20%. That is 10:1 influence (since $10,000 is one-tenth of $100,000). If your apartment suite acknowledges precisely the same 5%, you've quite recently earned $5,000 on an underlying $10,000 investment – a half return.

That is utilizing at work. Much the same as utilizing a physical switch, you've figured out how to lift up something substantial with less exertion. You profit by the thankfulness on the full estimation of the apartment suite despite the fact that the majority of the money used to get it was not yours yet the lender's.

Why Leveraging Your Home Makes Sense

We accept essential home possession is the one type of utilized investment that truly bodes well for the normal financial specialist. Utilizing amplifies the two increases and losses, so you should be cautious utilizing it if you would prefer not to get scorched – for instance, by purchasing on edge in the securities exchange.

However, when we're discussing your essential home, your dangers are lower since you're living in the home apparently as long as possible and have a high stake in making certain the regularly scheduled payments are made. Your dangers are lower, as well, if you purchase a home inside your budgetary safe place in any case.

Owning versus Leasing

Your month to month contract payment stays fixed, which gives you something you can depend on during your contributing years, and your home really turns out to be a piece of your general investment plan.

Home proprietorship is a constrained investment funds plan of sorts that permits you to develop your riches as the cost of the holdings increases in value. At last you can sell the home, cut back to something smaller, and utilize the rest of the value to help support your retirement.

The one alert we have is this: if you figure you may move areas over the present moment – for work reasons, state – you may wind up selling your home in a down market. Consequently you might need to hold up until you're sensibly secure in your activity before purchasing your home.

The Pros of Renting

Leasing gives you expanded adaptability with no long term duties. You have practically no obligation or cost for upkeep, home enhancements, or yard work. Your general expenses could possibly be lower than owning a home if you figure out how to lease inexpensively enough. And, over all that, you maintain a strategic distance from the requirement for a downpayment and a home loan by and large, subsequently permitting you to begin contributing sooner.

We positively trust it is conceivable to lease as opposed to possess and still retire early. If you keep rental costs sensibly low and invest considerably more money than you would have in any case in the business sectors to compensate for the value you won't have from owning a home, you can keep your life ultra-easy and still retire early. Contingent upon your way of life and where you live, leasing could be the correct response for you.

The Cons of Renting

Maybe the most noteworthy drawback of leasing is that you can't control the rental value, which will in general go up with time. Your landowner figures out what to charge, and in some cases the yearly increments can be sensational. A similar one-room loft we leased for $500 every month in 1991 presently leases for $1,200 every month – more than twofold. Lofts in places like New York City and San Francisco have presumably observed development factors a lot higher than twofold over that equivalent range of years.

By correlation, the expenses of home possession remain basically relentless with a fixed-rate contract. They may go up marginally because of little increments in protection and holdings charges, however the fundamental home loan rate itself stays fixed all through. This steadiness is a solace – something you can rely on during your contributing years.

Another drawback of leasing is that at last you don't have anything unmistakable to appear for all the rental payments you've made throughout the years. Maybe all that money just vanished like a phantom. Contrast this with home proprietorship, where you fabricate value as you proceed to can take that value with you once you sell your home. When we sold our home in 2007, we had the option to put $200,000 into a security reserve and utilize the other $100,000 to purchase a little condominium. Cutting back permitted us to expand our liquid investments, which was exactly what we required as early retirees depending on a salary stream from those investments.

A third drawback of leasing is that you can't adjust an investment holdings as you can a home. With rentals, what you see is regularly what you get, from paint hues to tooles to ground surface. In any case, with homes you can make changes both to the home itself and to the land it sits on, which thus can build the home's last worth.

Deducting Mortgage Interest

A last drawback of leasing is extremely a greater amount of an advantage to owning: with a home you find a workable pace intrigue payments from your separated assessments, which you can't do with a rental. It's no big surprise this has become the most loved assessment conclusion for many U.S. mortgage holders. A mortgage holder who burns through $12,000 in intrigue payments and $3,000 in holdings charges can deduct all $15,000 from his personal duties for the year.

The home loan derivation advantage is generally recognizable during the early long stretches of your credit when you're paying the most in intrigue. Since intrigue brings down every year on an amortization plan, one day you will arrive at a hybrid point where the standard reasoning ($12,200 in 2013 for a wedded couple indexing together) is worth more than the home loan intrigue conclusion.

15-Year versus 30-Year Mortgages

We suggest 15-year contracts as an especially solid match for the individuals who plan to retire early. You'll save a great deal on intrigue, and the 15 years coordinates pleasantly with an early retirement objective. We believe it's imperative to have your home totally paid off before you retire, and a 15-year contract lets you achieve that.

Nonetheless, financing costs are normally lower for a 15-year contract than they are for a 30-year contract as a result of the shorter advance length. The contrasts between the two models would be considerably increasingly sensational if we had considered, however it likewise would have made it harder to make a relevant comparison.

Looking at Monthly Payment Amounts

Let's look at the regularly scheduled payment sum. For a 30-year contract your regularly scheduled payment would be about $1,300, and for the 15-year contract it would be about $1,800. For a distinction of about $500 every month you can cut 15 years off your home loan.

Here's a reasonable inquiry: What if the contrast between the two payments is sufficient to put you outside the perfect scope of the 20/28 principle we prescribed before? We'll offer you a halfway response here, however make certain to likewise read the accompanying segment on "informal" 15-year contracts for what may be a superior other option.

We accept the advantages of doing a 15-year contract are so extraordinary contrasted with a 30-year contract that we would make a special case and prescribe you stretch for the 15-year contract as long as your regularly scheduled payments stayed inside the 28% most extreme required by the customary 28/36 guideline. That despite everything puts you inside the limits of what contract banks acknowledge as the passing reach for an advance, and at last it will get you to your retirement objective quicker.

Contrasting Total Interest Paid

As noted above, financing costs are normally lower for a 15-year contract than they are for a 30-year contract. However, in any event, when you expect the equivalent 5% pace of enthusiasm for the two home loans, note the immense contrast in the measure of all out intrigue paid: roughly $187,000 versus $85,000. That is a distinction of over $100,000 you don't need to pay if you go with a 15-year contract.

For the initial quite a long while of a 30-year contract, practically all you're paying is intrigue; you're not really making a scratch in the head. However, with a 15-year contract you make a perceptible scratch in the chief right from the earliest starting point. That implies your value becomes quicker, and your house is more your own and less the bank's.

If you should need to sell your home sooner than anticipated, your value stake will be more noteworthy with the 15-year contract. You can utilize that higher stake to put a more noteworthy downpayment on your next home, keeping your acquiring costs lower.

Looking at Total Holdings Tax Paid

The absolute holdings charge paid for a 15-year contract is half what it is really going after 30-year contract, yet this is somewhat deceptive. You would need to keep paying holdings charges on your home much after you took care of the 15-year contract, expecting you kept on living in it a short time later.

Under either situation, if you wound up remaining in the home for a long time, the all out holdings charge paid would be the equivalent. Nonetheless, if you sold the home tracking 15 years and cut back to a smaller holdings, your holdings charges starting now and into the foreseeable future would be similarly less.

Looking at PMI Paid

The above correlation does exclude private home loan protection, however if it did (i.e., because your downpayment was under 20%, in which case PMI is required), then the all out PMI paid for a 15-year credit would commonly be not exactly half what it is really going after 30-year advance. The explanation is that you arrive at 20% value in your home loan a lot quicker with the higher month to month head payments you're making on a 15-year credit, and subsequently you can drop the PMI sooner.

Looking at Total Amount Paid

When all is said and done, the aggregate sum paid in the above correlation is about $480,000 for a 30-year contract versus $332,000 for a 15-year contract. That is a distinction of about $150,000. We believe it merits an extra $500 every month in contract payments to save almost $150,000, isn't that right?

Coordinating Your Mortgage to Your Retirement Date

If you realize the specific retirement date you're going for, you can coordinate the length of your home loan to that date. For instance, if you intend to retire in 20 years, you could consider doing a 20-year contract.

Well, a similarly alluring option is to stay with the 15-year contract regardless of whether you realize you will retire in 20 years. That way the most recent five years before your retirement are totally contract free, permitting you to set aside up much more money during those years – or spend somewhat more unreservedly on movement and enjoyment as you ease towards retirement.

Renegotiating to a 15-Year Mortgage

If a 15-year contract isn't monetarily possible for you from the outset, you can generally renegotiate to one after you've lived in your home for a while. In any case, know renegotiating can include soak account charges. It's not surprising to pay 3% or a greater amount of your exceptional chief in renegotiating expenses. In this way renegotiating regularly doesn't bode well except if you're paying an a lot higher loan cost than you would somehow or another need to pay.

"Informal" 15-Year Mortgages

If the financing cost on your 30-year contract is as of now acceptably low, you can abstain from renegotiating accuses by staying of your 30-year contract however informally transforming it into a 15-year contract by squaring away the key quicker.

Making Extra Principal Payments

If you make additional payments towards the main every month (or on a fortnightly premise), that will have the impact of bringing down your general intrigue payments and lessening the term of the advance.

For example, if you pay an extra $100 every month towards the head on a $180,000 advance at 5% intrigue, your 30-year fixed-rate contract becomes basically a 25-year contract. An extra $200 every month makes it what might be compared to a 20-year contract. An extra $450 every month gets you what could be compared to a 15-year contract while never doing the official administrative work to make it one.

An additional advantage of this methodology is that you're not secured in the additional payments. If you should get yourself briefly jobless, you could ease off on making the additional payments for a while until you were re-utilized. You along these lines have less danger of defaulting on your credit.

The main drawback of this methodology is human instinct. It requires a decent plan of self-restraint to continue making the deliberate payments through various challenges, after quite a long time after year. Well, if you are adequately propelled to retire early and have the control it takes, this can be an extraordinary solution.

Prepayment Calculators

Home loan amortization number crunchers like the one at HSH.com let you run distinctive head prepayment situations. Simply plug various sums into the "Month to month Additional Principal Prepayment Amount" box and hit "Figure." You can rapidly observe the consequences of making various prepayments, including the all out intrigue you will pay and the result date. This permits you to tailor your prepayment technique to coordinate your needs.

Waiting in Your Home

Numerous individuals exchange up from their first home, utilizing it as a venturing stone to a greater home, then exadjusting up once more to a much greater one. Why, precisely? When you think about the vitality and cost engaged with pressing and unloading, rebuilding and refurnishing, repainting and redesigning, and purchasing then purchasing again to suit the requirements and measurements of each greater home, it makes you wonder what it's supportive of.

We recommend rather you wait in your first home. Keep your life less difficult and your needs smaller by remaining in one spot. Increment your current home's estimation by making enhancements to it all around. If you have no other decision however to move in view of your activity or some other need, then try moving sideways and purchasing a house that is practically identical to the one you as of now have as opposed to upsizing.

Exadjusting up for increasingly more home is counterproductive in case you're looking for early retirement. You will probably limit your costs while boosting your investment funds. Keeping your lodging costs as low as sensibly conceivable will let you accomplish that objective with significantly less trouble.

If you have children or plan on having them, attempt to purchase a first home large enough to oblige them directly from the earliest starting point so you don't need to move to a greater home later on. Obviously nobody has a precious stone ball and everything you can do is your best. Here and there guardians have no other decision however to purchase a greater home if they wind up having a bigger number of children than anticipated.

If you purchase a home that wind up being too large for your needs, you can generally think about inventive approaches to utilize that additional room to further your own potential profit.

Is a Renter Right for You?

If you're willing to engage the probability of having a leaseholder, then consider first how your house is planned. Does it take into consideration a decent lot of security for you and your leaseholder? Does it offer a different passage? Are there independent washrooms with showers? Would you be able to set up a small scale kitchen in the piece of the home you'll be leasing? The more you can limit the need to impart space to your leaseholder, the simpler it will be for all gatherings.

We realize numerous individuals feel emphatically about not having any desire to impart their home to any other person, and we perceive this might possibly be a correct alternative for you. In case you're awkward with the idea of having a tenant, maybe you can think about to different ways you could utilize any additional room in your house that is simply sitting unfilled. Possibly you can set up a little independent investment or something to that affect, for instance. Let your imaginative energies stream while thinking about various methods for getting a little extra salary over your customary compensations. Indeed, even some additional salary can go far when you're endeavouring relentlessly to live underneath your methods.

Cutting back When You Retire

You might need to consider offering your greater home and cutting back to a smaller home or apartment suite once you retire. As we addressed before, this permits you to take a bit of the value developed in your home and put it in a progressively liquid resource, for example, a security finance.

Liquid resources are progressively usable resources for early retirees. You can remove $10,000 from a security store and use it for everyday costs once you retire, however you can't remove $10,000 from your home in the equivalent simple way. You'd either need to take out a home value advance (which means returning into obligation) or lease all or a piece of your home (which can be badly planned) to access the equivalent $10,000. In any case, if you scale back after you retire, you can take the straggling leftovers and put it in a shared store offering both liquidity and a pay stream.

One of the extraordinary advantages of home proprietorship under current law is that when it comes time to sell your essential home, you owe no assessments at all on the first $250,000 of capital increases (or $500,000 for couples). This can be a gift from heaven in case you're searching for some additional money with which to pad your savings once you retire.

Obviously another alternative is to purchase a smaller home or townhouse directly from the beginning and remain in it considerably after you retire. If you choose to move to an alternate area, you could generally exchange sideways, purchasing another home or apartment suite for about a similar cost. The advantages of this methodology are, it downplays your home loan (i.e., you never purchased more home than you required), your holdings charges are lower, and your utility expenses are lower since your area is less.

If you go the apartment suite course, make certain to mull over month to month HOA expenses. You'll need to ensure they're as low as sensibly conceivable since they are what might be compared to paying rent every month. An astounding plan on a townhouse can appear to be less staggering once you factor in these charges.

The Real Cost of a New Car

The normal cost for another vehicle nowadays is over $30,000. If rather than another vehicle for $30,000, you were to purchase a pre-owned one for $10,000; the remaining $20,000 could finance an entire year of contributing for retirement. In case you're a couple and every one of you chooses to purchase a trade-in vehicle for $10,000 rather than another one for $30,000 that is $40,000 additional that could be put towards retirement investment funds.

Presently let's guess you have a 20-year retirement plan and your objective is to taken care of $20,000 every year by and large. That is $400,000 complete you have to invest, with the remainder of your portfolio's development originating from exacerbating. The $40,000 you could have saved by purchasing two trade-in vehicles rather than two new ones speaks to one-tenth of your complete investment sum.

That is the genuine expense of another vehicle. You could be exadjusting the opportunity to retire quite a long while prior.

Self-Financing

In case you're purchasing a trade-in vehicle for $10,000 rather than another one for $30,000, the probability of self-financing turns out to be substantially more achievable. You could begin a vehicle reserve and set aside the entire sum early, paying for the vehicle in real money and subsequently staying away from the need to pay enthusiasm on a vehicle credit.

Regardless of whether you just figure out how to set aside a large portion of the sum, an advance of $5,000 is less scary to take care of (and repay rapidly) than a credit of $10,000 or more. The fewer obligations you have hanging over you the better.

Sharing One Car or Going Carless

For some individuals a vehicle is a need during their working years, yet if you can get by without one and depend on open vehicle rather, that would be preferable. When I worked in Denver for various years, I brought an express transport into the city every day not exclusively to bring down my costs yet in addition to maintain a strategic distance from the cerebral pains of city driving.

Anybody living in a significant city with a metro framework ought to consider managing without a vehicle just to maintain a strategic distance from the high cost of leaving. If you just endeavour out of the city on uncommon events, consider leasing a vehicle exactly when you need one. It would in all likelihood be less expensive than owning.

In case you're a couple and one of you is sufficiently fortunate to be inside biking separation of work, then you might have the option to get by with one vehicle rather than two. Not exclusively will your expenses go down, yet you'll get some great exercise every day.

Purchasing a Used Car

Purchasing a trade-in vehicle isn't especially dangerous if you get your work done first. Equipped with information you can turn into an educated purchaser. We recommend you start with Kelly Blue Book (kbb.com) or Edmunds (edmunds.com), which can supply you with the evaluated value extend for the vehicle you're keen on purchasing. Carfax (carfax.com) lets you beware of a trade-in's vehicle history. Basically enter the VIN or the state and tag number to pull up the index. The present expense is $35 for one vehicle, $45 for up to five, and $50 for boundless reports inside 30 days.

A vehicle investigation from a nearby specialist is every now and again offered requiring little to no effort as an impetus for future business. It's keen to have a repairman take a gander at a trade-in vehicle first before you get it.

Utilizing Craigslist to Buy or Sell a Car

Think about purchasing or selling your vehicle on Craigslist (craigslist.com). The site's free classifieds offer a vigorously utilized discussion for purchasing and selling utilized vehicles and pretty much everything else under the sun. We sold our two vehicles in less than seven days in the wake of posting promotions on the site and had the option to get the value we needed. We additionally found our current trade-in vehicle by means of a posting on Craigslist. In case you're a solitary lady, we would prescribe carrying somebody with you when purchasing or selling for security reasons.

Make certain to post quality photographs with your promotion – it has a major effect as far as your prosperity rate. You can repost your promotion like clockwork to move it to the highest point of the line, which merits doing since it builds your perceivability to imminent purchasers.

Purchasing versus Renting

We don't suggest renting a vehicle as opposed to getting one. The long term cost of renting is for all intents and purposes in every case more than the expense of purchasing. It makes sense when you consider it. If you buy a solitary vehicle and drive it for 10 years or more, you will improve cost-wise than if you rent a few autos over that equivalent timeframe.

A great many people we realize who rent their vehicles turn them in each a few years so they're continually driving what adds up to another or near new vehicle. In any case, there's a cost to be paid for that profit. You once in a while get something in vain right now.

What confounds numerous individuals, and naturally along these lines, is that month to month rent payments are ordinarily 30% to 60% not exactly ordinary vehicle advance payments. This appears to be a lot from the start, however it's tricky because month to month rent payments never end as long as you are renting the vehicle.

When you take care of an ordinary vehicle credit, you possess the vehicle through and through. Other than upkeep and fix costs, you can drive the vehicle payment free for a considerable length of time to desire as long as it remains street commendable. Your credit costs are successfully spread out over the whole possession time of the vehicle. Along these lines, despite the fact that a customary advance payment may appear to be higher when contrasted with a month to month rent payment, it's in reality a lot of lower when you consider.

Paying for Car Repairs

Consider fix costs cautiously before choosing to exchange your older vehicle for a fresher one. The facts confirm that fix costs are higher for older vehicles, however every additional year you can crush out of your current vehicle is one more year without month to month credit payments or a major capital use to purchase a more up to date one.

Paying a high vehicle fix bill can be difficult because it hits at the same time and frequently out of nowhere, yet it is less excruciating if you intellectually spread the expense out over all the additional months you'll find a good pace vehicle once it's fixed.

Obviously, sooner or later the transmission may blow or some other fix cost might be high to the point that it never again gets sense to empty more money-flow into a vehicle that has practically zero worth left to it. By then it's reasonable to persuade it to retire and search for a substitution. Kelly Blue Book (kbb.com) can assist you with deciding your vehicle's present worth and whether you should jump on costly fixes.

Chapter Nine

Determine Your Income Needs As A Retiree

Making sense of how a lot of money you're probably going to require on a yearly premise to some degree far off future is no simple issue. However, you can begin with this basic reason: your costs will very likely be lower than they are presently.

Why? Well, first of all, you won't have to invest for retirement any more once you're retired, clearly, so those "costs" will leave. And, you won't make contract payments anymore, and any costs related with bringing up kids and sending them off to school will never again apply. Certain business related costs will drop away once you never again need to make the day by day drive. Noteworthy home and yard enhancements ought to be a relic of past times. Also, your duties will more likely than not go down contrasted with what you're paying at this point.

Then again, your medicinal services expenses may increment to some degree, just as your movement and relaxation costs. Then there's swelling, which ceaselessly consumes the estimation of your dollar a seemingly endless amount of time after year. Swelling adds an entirely different measurement to the conversation.

We'll discuss every one of these elements in a minute, yet first we'd prefer to examine the solid contrasts of assessment that exist about how best to decide your future yearly pay needs.

Two Methods for Calculating Future Income

One methodology touted by numerous monetary and protection firms is to begin with your present pay then increase that pay by 70% or 80% to decide the sum you're probably going to require later on. We think this strategy is on a very basic level imperfect. It will in general outcome in an overestimate that makes individuals think they have to save a greater savings than they truly do. It's a given this advantages the equivalent budgetary firms that suggest it, since it implies more money streaming into their coffers.

Since compensations will in general be at their most elevated towards the finish of an individual's profession, a conundrum circumstance can bring about which ever more significant compensations lead to ever higher assessments of future needs, which thus drives the apparent requirement for an ever greater savings. The entirety of this prompts the conviction that you have to continue working, continue saving, and continue endeavouring. However, in all actuality, current salary has little to do with the amount you'll require once you retire. Let's utilize our own model as an a valid example.

Towards the finish of our working years we were making the most we had ever earned, as will in general be the situation. Firms prescribing the salary way to deal with ascertaining your retirement needs commonly propose you take the normal of your last ten years of yearly pay. They instruct you to increase that sum by 70% and 80% to get a range speaking to the low end and high finish of what you're probably going to require to keep up your present way of life in retirement.

If you are forcefully putting something aside for early retirement, then the after-effects of the 70-80 strategy will in general be especially slanted. An enormous piece of your salary is going towards investments and is in this manner off the table regarding what you're really living on at present.

Anybody pushing hard to retire early is probably going to be driven off track by utilizing current salary as the methods for deciding the amount they'll require once they retire.

Rather we prescribe you start with current costs to decide your retirement needs. Genuine everyday costs in the present day give you a superior interpretation of what you'll require not far off, when you have subtracted out the ones that never again apply and have made fitting alterations for inflation.

It's especially critical to get the yearly retirement salary number right since it nourishes easily into the count of how enormous your savings should be. The distinction between having the option to live on $40,000 every year and $80,000 every year is the contrast between expecting to set aside a savings of $1 million and $2 million. Consider what number of additional long stretches of work it would take to hoard an additional million dollars in investment funds. Along these lines the yearly retirement pay gauge gets amplified as far as its latent capacity sway on your life and the choices you make about your own future.

Making an Initial Estimate Based on Current Expenses

Let's start by investigating your present everyday costs. Suppose you and your companion presently have a consolidated gross pay of $100,000, or $75,000 net after duties. Presently, utilizing wide brushstrokes, we should wipe out a couple of the significant costs you likely won't have once you retire.

First of all, the home loan will be paid off when you retire, so that's, state, $1,250 every month or $15,000 every year you won't need to stress over. Maybe you've additionally been taking care of $3,000 every year for your children's advanced degree. And, suppose you've distinguished another $1,000 every year in extra costs identified with kids, employments, home redesign, yard support, etc that you feel genuinely certain will never again apply once you're retired.

At last, suppose you're in your essential contributing years and have been storing $20,000 every year into your retirement reserves. Obviously, that "cost" will never again be there once you're retired. So:

$100,000 (consolidated gross salary)

- $25,000 (charges at 25%)
- $15,000 (contract payments)
- $3,000 (children's school support)
- $1,000 (misc. costs identified with kids, employments, home upgrades, and so on.)
- $20,000 (retirement investments) $36,000 (balanced total compensation)

This speculative situation proposes you and your life partner could be making due with as little as $36,000 net every year if not for contract payments, additional costs related with children and work, and the need to put something aside for school and retirement. That is some truly economical living you're doing when you think of it as that way.

In any case, presently the pendulum needs to swing the other way. You've done some subtraction, presently you have to do some inflation. To make an exact evaluation of the amount you'll require once you retire, you need to add money back in to represent swelling, charges, and possibly higher human services costs in retirement.

We won't attempt to represent expanded travel costs right now they can shift such a great amount starting with one individual then onto the next, yet you might need to cushion your gauge marginally higher if you hope to travel seriously once retired.

Adjusting for Inflation

Inflation on an across the nation premise ascends by a normal of generally 3% every year as per the Consumer Price Index, which gauges the expense of a container of basic merchandise and enterprises Americans purchase (nourishment, apparel, lodging, restorative consideration, vitality, and so on.). The CPI is a national normal of costs, however dependent on our own experience we think 3% is somewhat high for ascertaining your own swelling rate. If you live deliberately, you can shield inflation from having as solid of an effect on your life as it would have on the economy all in all.

For example, the cost of seeing a film in an auditorium may have gone up to $12 per ticket, yet that doesn't mean you can't settle on the cognizant choice to keep a watch out a similar motion picture at home for a dollar. And, on the grounds that a café raises its lunch cost to $20 doesn't mean you can't settle on the cognizant choice to eat elsewhere more moderately. You may do takeout for a large portion of the cost or make lunch at home for even less. So while we can't disregard the impacts of inflation, we can alleviate its belongings somewhat by settling on keen choices in our own lives.

We think an individual swelling pace of 2% is nearer to the

imprint than 3%, and that is the number we'll use here. Yet, remember high swelling can pop up whenever and represent a difficult issue for retirees on a fixed pay. Watch out for what's going on in reality and alter your counts and manners of thinking likewise.

In view of an individual inflation pace of 2%, to have what could be compared to $36,000 in the present dollars you'd need $36,000 + 2% = $36,720 one year from now. The year after that you'd need $36,720 + 2% = $37,454, etc. In 15 years' time, to have the purchasing power $36,000 gives you today, you'd need $48,451. For the wellbeing of simplicity we should gather the number together to $49,000.

Altering for Taxes in Retirement

The net sum our theoretical couple will require in retirement is $49,000. In any case, when they pull back money from their retirement accounts they'll ordinarily be pulling back gross continues and may need to pay some measure of annual tax on that sum.

For the time being let's expect 10% annual assessments and add $5,444 to the $49,000 to land at a gross pay of $54,444. (If you're keen on figuring it out, partition the net measure of $49,000 by 90% to land at the gross sum.) For easyness' purpose we'll gather the number together to $55,000.

Modifying for Health Care in Retirement

You may likewise need to include some money in for conceivably higher medicinal services costs in retirement. Starting at 2014, the Affordable Care Act will make human services substantially more moderate for early retirees on a financial limit. The impacts of this new enactment are huge enough that we're just going to add $1,000 to our speculative couple's aggregate, and that is for the most part to represent higher out-of-pocket costs related with things like dental and vision care that aren't really secured under the new law.

Remember you're likely not paying zero dollars for human services right now. Regardless of whether your manager covers you, you're in all likelihood paying something into the framework. As indicated by the Employer Health Profits 201 Survey by the Kaiser Family Foundation, for instance, workers with family inclusion invest, by and large, $344 every month ($4,129 yearly) towards their medical coverage premiums. The $1,000 we're including is top of whatever sum our theoretical couple is as of now paying for wellbeing and dental consideration during their working years.

Chapter Ten

Your Nest Egg

Maybe the idea has jumped out at you, what precisely establishes my savings? Is the value in my home a piece of it? And, shouldn't something be said about the money in my 401(k) and IRA that I don't anticipate contacting until after I'm 59½? Does that check towards my savings when I'm attempting to decide what amount is protected to pull back in the underlying long periods of my initial retirement?

These are reasonable inquiries and ones we considered ourselves as we were approaching early retirement. We'll put forth a valiant effort to give some direction dependent on our own contemplating these issues both when resigning.

What Constitutes Your Nest Egg?

Your retirement fund should comprise just of fluid resources, for example, stocks, securities, and money, not illiquid resources, for example, land. Land is more diligently to sell and progressively lumbering to work with if you need to create money for current everyday costs. All things considered, if you plan on scaling back your home once you resign, whatever sum you won't requirement for homebuying purposes later on can be transformed into fluid resources that do check towards your savings.

What amount of Your Home Counts?

We prescribe you put aside a part of your home's value (say, between one quarter and one half) for future land purposes. This sum can be applied either to a scaled back home or to taking care of rental expenses any place you may happen to live on the planet if you decide not to claim a home for a while. In any case, you're on the ball if you don't need to subtract this sum out of your savings once you resign.

Are Your 401(k) and Roth IRA Assets Part of Your Nest Egg?

Choosing whether 401(k) and Roth IRA resources are fluid or illiquid in the prior year's you can get to them without punishment is honestly something of a hazy area. Here are our musings on the issue, in spite of the fact that others may sensibly oppose this idea.

We suggest you do incorporate 401(k) and Roth IRA sums while computing your savings, regardless of whether you plan on depending exclusively on the money in your assessable index in the years before turning 59½. The stock, security, and shared store resources in these indexes truly are fluid and could be sold for money rapidly if need be. Obviously you will likely leave them immaculate for quite a long time to come since you would somehow or another need to take care of a punishment charge for getting to them rashly, yet they are all things considered still fluid in nature.

Because you pick (shrewdly) to depend entirely on the assessable part of your fluid resources during your initial retirement years doesn't mean the other expense advantaged fluid resources don't exist. They do exist and in certainty are probably going to develop in the years to come, giving you a constant flow of salary when all is good and well. Not calculating them into your retirement fund is disregard a critical and ever-expanding segment of your portfolio.

Utilizing the 4% Rule to Calculate Your Nest Egg

When you've decided your yearly retirement pay needs, the tracking stage is simple. You can utilize what's known as the 4% rule to gauge the savings you'll require to securely create that sum. We should begin with $56,000, the yearly retirement salary sum from our model in the past section. Utilizing a variety of the 4% rule called the "Rule of 25," you can play out a fast back-of-the-napkin retirement fund computation. Basically increase the salary sum by 25 to decide the size of the retirement fund you'll require. For instance:

$56,000 (yearly retirement salary) x 25 = $1.4 million savings

It's as direct as that. A savings of $1.4 million will create a yearly retirement pay of $56,000 for our theoretical couple. Note that separating the salary sum by 4% will get you a similar outcome as duplicating by 25. The two methodologies are numerically the equivalent as far as furnishing you with an answer with regards to the size of the savings you need.

Maybe a simpler method to envision how the 4% rule functions is to begin with the savings sum itself and duplicate by 4% to decide the yearly salary sum it will securely produce, as follows:

$500,000 retirement fund x 4% = $20,000 salary every year

$750,000 retirement fund x 4% = $30,000 salary every year

$1,000,000 retirement fund x 4% = $40,000 salary every year

$1,250,000 retirement fund x 4% = $50,000 salary every year

$1,500,000 retirement fund x 4% = $60,000 salary every year

$1,750,000 retirement fund x 4% = $70,000 salary every year

$2,000,000 retirement fund x 4% = $80,000 salary every year

Try not to be astounded if the savings sum you ascertain is bigger than you were foreseeing. Swelling can have that impact. Yet, remember your compensation will likewise be staying aware of – and ideally outpacing – swelling over the coming 15 to 20 years, so what may appear as though an unthinkably huge number presently should feel progressively feasible as the years pass and your pay increments. Exacerbating will likewise help you in arriving at your objective, giving you a tailwind in the later long periods of your plan.

Why Is 4% a Safe Withdrawal Amount?

You might be pondering, Why 4%? Why not pretty much than that? Doesn't 4% appear to be misleadingly low? Wouldn't you be able to take out, say, 6% and still be alright? Furthermore, how safe will be protected when individuals reveal to you 4% is a sheltered add up to pull back? Let's attempt to answer a couple of these inquiries.

The Original 4% Rule

Most money related organizers nowadays concur on some variety of the 4% rule. As initially figured by William Bengen, an ensured budgetary organizer in the mid 1990s, the standard states you can securely pull back 4% of your savings in your first year of retirement and increment that sum every year from that point for swelling without an excess of danger of draining your retirement fund more than 30 years.

Suppose you have a $1 million savings. As per the customary utilization of the 4% rule, your first year of retirement you could take out $1 million x 4% = $40,000. One year from now, changing for inflation (suppose it's at 2%), you could take out $40,000 + 2% = $40,800. The year from that point onward, if swelling were at 3%, you could take out $40,800 + 3% = $42,024, etc. That is the 4% rule at its generally fundamental.

Financial specialists have done cautious verifiable demonstrating and run broad calculations (called Monte Carlo reenactments) to come to the end result that 4% is a sensibly protected add up to pull back from your portfolio every year. Bengen himself reasoned that drawing down just 1% more than that every year – that is, 5% in addition to inflation changes – brought about a 30% possibility of a retiree's savings being exhausted too early. For the normal retiree that is just too high a risk.

At or Near the Limit of Safety

Drawn out downturns in the market can unleash destruction with a investment portfolio, particularly in the early long periods of one's retirement, and any great dependable guideline needs to represent that plausibility. A couple of long periods of negative returns, joined with higher than ordinary withdrawals, could exhaust a portfolio to where it can never again support itself however rather starts a moderate winding towards zero.

While the securities exchange may restore a normal of 9% over the long term, it tends to be everywhere temporarily, and the 4% rule is intended to make up for that. It's additionally useful to recollect that posted yearly returns are commonly pre-charge and don't represent inflation. A 9% return is more like a 7% genuine return subsequent to considering in swelling, and it's even lower than that in the wake of calculating in charges.

When these issues are contemplated, 4% ends up being the rate that is at or close to the furthest reaches of security. Almost all monetary models concur that your retirement fund is at genuine danger of being exhausted too early if you are reliably pulling back 6% or more, so keep your withdrawals in the 4% to 5% territory if you need to stand a sensible possibility of seeing your portfolio last longer than you do.

Tragically there is nothing of the sort as ironclad wellbeing with regards to contributing, just relative security. Under horrendous financial conditions it is conceivable to exhaust your portfolio regardless of whether you just took out 4% every year. In any case, all the better you can do is fail on the preservationist side so the chances are in support of you and perceive there are no assurances either throughout everyday life or in contributing.

Changing the 4% Rule to Address Limitations

Obviously the 4% rule is just a general guideline and not a definite science, however it fills in as a decent budgetary measuring stick for deciding the rough size of the savings you'll require. We think it works best when, similar to any general guideline, it is applied with a solid portion of presence of mind. The standard as initially figured has some significant confinements, so we prescribe you use it yet in a changed manner as portrayed underneath.

Is Thirty Years Enough?

The central issue with the 4% rule as initially explained is that it was just intended to apply to 30 years of retirement living. However, with individuals living longer and resigning prior, this suspicion never again remains constant for each situation. You may need to finance 40 or even 50 years of retirement living.

Our answer for this issue is to successfully kill the

programmed swelling alteration highlight incorporated with the first guideline. If you don't alter for inflation consistently or make just negligible changes – particularly in the early long stretches of your retirement – then you are supporting your wagers for a solid investment portfolio that is probably going to outlive you.

Inflation has been so low in the course of recent years that we have had the option to go six years so far without expecting to modify our yearly withdrawal sums. Just presently are we starting to see a genuine contrast in our purchasing power. By limiting swelling alterations, we give our portfolio a superior possibility of continuing itself as well as becoming over the long term. This builds the chances it will be there to help us 40 or even 50 years down the line if vital.

Concerning inflation in our later years, we believe we can depend on future government managed savings payments to help with that. Truth be told that is actually how we consider government managed savings: as a support against inflation in the far off future.

Tweaking Withdrawals Based on Actual Conditions

Another issue with the 4% rule as generally planned is that it makes no endeavour to represent changes in spending conduct because of large picture changes in the economy. The standard is applied indiscriminately, fundamentally. Regardless of whether you are in the profundities of a downturn or at the statures of a thundering positively trending business sector, it generally prescribes you pull back the very same sum every year (other than making up for swelling). This makes it easy to apply yet unyielding with regards to moving with the punches that the money related markets at times toss at you.

In light of this worry, numerous financial analysts advocate beginning with the 4% rule yet tweaking your withdrawals from year to year dependent on real economic situations. This sounds good to us. If the financial exchange is performing amazingly a seemingly endless amount of time after year, then you shouldn't feel obliged as far as possible yourself to 4% in addition to the swelling rate. In such a circumstance you may be justified in taking out 6% of your savings (or more) in a given year – as long as it doesn't turn into your new standard. After an especially decent series of years, you may spend too much on that around the globe trip you've constantly longed for before coming back to an increasingly typical withdrawal rate the next year.

Then again, if the economy is in a profound and delayed downturn, then aimlessly applying the 4% rule – which generally would call for you to expand your withdrawal sums so as to represent inflation – would be sketchy, best case scenario. You may wind up physically debilitating the wellbeing of your portfolio and diminishing its odds of endurance over the long term. Under such conditions it is shrewd to pull back under 4% (or if nothing else not modify for inflation) so as to shield your portfolio from further disintegration. Expanding the adaptability of the 4% rule in such a style offers a progressively realistic, eyes-all the way open way to deal with drawing down your retirement fund.

Accomplishing a Self-Sustaining Portfolio

A self-continuing portfolio is your general monetary objective once you resign. A portfolio that is developing at a moderate pace is a portfolio equipped for staying aware of inflation and furnishing you with a somewhat higher yearly salary as the years pass. Altering the 4% rule by 1) killing programmed inflation alterations for manual changes, and 2) tweaking your withdrawal rates dependent on real economic situations ought to permit you to accomplish this objective.

Utilizing Retirement Calculators

You can utilize online retirement number crunchers related to the 4% rule to decide the inexact size of the savings you'll require. We referenced one we especially like at daveramsey.com (under the "Tooles" tab). It makes a bar graph indicating how your money mixes from year to year and lets you plug in various qualities to explore different avenues regarding various situations.

Another clever online tool is the Retirement Nest Egg Calculator on Vanguard's site. (Simply type "Vanguard savings number cruncher" into Google and it will furnish you with the connection, which is somewhat long and lumbering). The adding machine runs 5,000 free Monte Carlo reenactments with simply the snap of a catch.

Sliding bars lets you indicate four information focuses: 1) how long your portfolio needs to last, 2) your present portfolio balance, 3) the amount you hope to spend from your portfolio every year, and 4) the level of stocks, bonds, and money in your portfolio. In light of this data it figures the likelihood of your portfolio enduring the quantity of years you've indicated. In case you're not happy with the outcomes, you can change the sliding bars to investigate distinctive what if situations.

Chapter Eleven

Create A Long Term Investment Plan

When making a long term investment plan it assists with having the option to plainly express your objective so there is no perplexity about where you are going. For instance: "I need to resign in 15 years and have a retirement fund of $1.5 million so as to create $60,000 in pay every year." To have the option to assemble an objective articulation like this you have to work in reverse, generally, and complete three stages

1. Estimate your yearly pay needs once you resign.
2. Calculate your savings dependent on these yearly pay needs.
3. Put together a point by point plan sketching out how long it will take to set aside your savings and the amount you'll have to invest every year.

This part handles the exceptionally significant advance. You may as of now have an underlying feeling of the quantity of years until your objective retirement date, yet finishing this progression will assist you with refining that understanding. Before the finish of it you'll have a greatly improved handle on the amount you'll have to put every year so as to achieve your objective in the ideal number of years.

What the Historical Index Shows

You need to make presumptions when getting ready for what's to come, there's just no chance to get around it. For whatever length of time that your suspicions have a premise indeed – and over the present moment as well as over the long term – you're on generally strong ground. However, it would be a misstep to expect 20% annualized securities exchange returns since you're sufficiently fortunate to encounter a 20% return at whatever year, or even in a series of years. Why? Since the authentic index just doesn't bolster it.

What the chronicled index supports is the likelihood of financial exchange returns in the 8% to 10% territory over the long term. Does that mean you're unquestionably going to get those profits during the years in which you are effectively contributing? No, obviously not. However, you must beginning some place, and as great a spot to begin as any is with the indexed returns of the financial exchange over a significant stretch of time – state, from before the Great Depression in 1929 to the present day.

Getting a precise read on chronicled financial exchange performance is a shockingly dubious thing in its own right. You'd figure everybody would concur looking back, for instance, on what the annualized returns have been for the S&P 500. All things considered, the S&P 500 is a index of the 500 greatest and best-promoted organizations in the U.S. In any case, various sites post marginally unique annualized returns for that year, albeit most are in harsh understanding.

The Problem With Using Simple Averages

Utilizing the basic normal appears to be sufficiently direct, isn't that right? However, it isn't generally the best methodology. We should take a gander at an extraordinary guide to delineate. Suppose you have $10,000 put resources into a specific stock and you make 100% on your interest in the main year. That implies you made $10,000 on your investment, leaving you with another aggregate of $20,000.

Presently suppose you lose half of that investment the tracking year. That is lost $10,000, returning you right where you began at $10,000. Your genuine annualized gain is zero since you began and finished at a similar dollar sum. However, the easy normal would propose your yearly return was 25%. Why? Since (100% increase - half loss) ÷ 2 = 25%. We instinctively observe this doesn't bode well – and that is the place compound yearly development rates (CAGR) prove to be useful.

Why Compound Annual Growth Rates Are More Reliable

A compound yearly development rate basically shows the rate at which a investment would have developed if it developed at a relentless rate. By utilizing the geometric mean as opposed to the number juggling mean it gives a more genuine image of real returns. Shockingly, figuring the CAGR is no simple issue except if you're a math virtuoso or happen to have a budgetary mini-computer available.

Figuring a fragmentary example isn't something you can without much of a stretch do on a standard number cruncher. Notwithstanding, sites like moneychimp.com and investopedia.com now offer CAGR number crunchers you can utilize. For our motivations, the significant thing to comprehend is that figurings dependent on CAGR give an increasingly exact evaluation of long term annualized returns, and that is the thing that our emphasis is on here.

As per moneychimp.com, the annualized return of the S&P 500 from 1871 to 2012 dependent on compound yearly development rates is 8.92%. The CAGR is generally a percent or two not exactly the easy normal (which you may review was 10.60%). Swelling balanced annualized returns over this equivalent period were 6.71% dependent on the CAGR.

What Annual Rate of Return Should You Use?

The S&P 500 is a sensible intermediary for the whole U.S. financial exchange, so it is reasonable for state that, as time goes on, the securities exchange has had an annualized return of around 9% and an inflation balanced return of roughly 7%. If you need to anticipate the future, you could do more awful than putting together your presumptions with respect to these rates.

Presently in case you're hopeful essentially, you can expect financial exchange returns of 10% or perhaps even 11% every year and still be pretty much in scope of what the verifiable index bolsters. However, going a lot higher than that may begin to look more like unrealistic reasoning than faithful arranging.

When assembling your own monetary plan for the future, we propose you utilize a rate pace of somewhere in the range of 8% and 10% every year if you are putting basically in the securities exchange, with 9% being the conspicuous centre ground presumption. Some will say this is excessively high, others excessively low, however at any rate it is in the ball park. Remember a 9% return depends on putting the heft of your money in stocks during your essential contributing years. If you wish to invest all the more minimalistically, with securities making up 25% or a greater amount of your portfolio, you might need to expect a somewhat lower yearly pace of return.

You might be pondering whether you should utilize swelling balanced returns when making presumptions about future investment development. (Swelling balanced returns are for the most part around two rate focuses lower than unadjusted returns.) with respect to your own investment plan we would state no, and here's the reason: you previously considered in inflation (i.e., by including 2% every year) while computing your future retirement pay needs. That implies your retirement fund has just been balanced upwards to represent swelling. Altering yearly returns downwards too is representing swelling twice.

Regardless of whether the suspicions you make about future securities exchange returns aren't absolutely right (and there's a decent possibility they won't be), the insignificant actuality that you have made an plan and clung to it implies you're on top of things and without a doubt happier than you would have been something else.

Market Resilience

It's a solace to recollect that the securities exchange has endure and flourished in spite of such disastrous occasions as the Stock Market Crash of 1929, the resulting Great Depression, and two World Wars. It places into viewpoint the worries of our own time and causes us to understand the business sectors are shockingly flexible over the long term. Returns might be compliment than we might want, or even negative for a while, yet over the long term the business sectors have consistently bobbed back and substantiated themselves very strong.

For anybody simply starting to invest today, it's additionally something of a solace to understand that the Great Recession has wrung some risk out of the business sectors. During the five-year time frame from 2008 to 2012, the S&P 500 returned simply

1.63% dependent on the compound yearly development rate (or -0.17% when balanced for swelling). This proposes stocks may offer a superior incentive than they did before the downturn, which could look good for what's to come. Markets may (and we underline may) beat in the years to come, aligning yearly returns more with long term chronicled averages.

Setting up Your Investment Spreadsheet

Since you've gotten an opportunity to analyze some speculative spreadsheet models and consider the likely paces of return you should utilize, it's a great opportunity to set up your own investment spreadsheet. This spreadsheet will fill in as your all-inclusive strategy going ahead. It will follow your assessable, 401(k), and Roth IRA investments and will incorporate a Grand Total segment so you can rapidly observe where you remain toward the finish of every year.

When your spreadsheet is set up, you should simply return to it once every year to survey how you're doing against plan. You'll refresh it by then to incorporate real outcomes rather than gauges for the year simply past. That will build the precision and pertinence of your plan going ahead.

We ask you not to avoid this progression regardless of whether the word spreadsheet gives you chills. We guarantee to keep it basic. All the more significantly, we offer a spreadsheet format on the web if you'd lean toward not assemble the layout without any preparation. (Also, for what reason would you?)

To profit yourself of this easy route, essentially visit our site at wherewebe.com and download the Excel spreadsheet layout under the "Early Retirement" tab. It's a similar format we present here, and it as of now has the entirety of the segments and recipes set up for you. There's even a supportive guidance sheet on a different tab inside the archive.

You'll despite everything need to go into the spreadsheet itself, obviously, and physically enter the dollar sums you hope to invest every year, except this is a easy matter of information passage. When this is done, the spreadsheet is custom fitted to your circumstance and you can start tweaking it to play with various investment situations.

There are noteworthy tax preferences to 401(k) and Roth IRA accounts that make them important to for all intents and purposes each individual getting ready for retirement.

Any progressions you make to the spreadsheet are right away reflected in the reality. For example, if you change the yearly pace of come back from 9% to 10%, you can immediately watch your sums increment. If you modify your assessable investment sums from $5,000 to $10,000 every year, you can perceive how your retirement fund at the base of the spreadsheet promptly becomes greater.

Try not to feel constrained by the example numbers remembered for the spreadsheet; they are essentially illustrative and have not any more bearing without anyone else reality than they do on yours.

Make Your Spreadsheet a Living Document

We urge you to think about your end-all strategy not as a solitary archive unchangeable however as an adaptable report that can be adjusted and tweaked voluntarily. The thought is to play with various situations until you land at one that feels right to you. If your material circumstance transforms, you can change the spreadsheet to mirror your new reality, in this manner keeping it present and pertinent to your life. Prior cycles of your plan can generally be put something aside for the index, yet ensure the current year's plan is as precise to your certifiable circumstance as could be allowed.

A spreadsheet with no pertinence to your genuine honestly misses the general purpose. If you figured you could save $10,000 every year except it rapidly becomes evident you can't, don't forsake your plan by and large. Rather, just change it to make it fit what you can do. Try dividing your objective to $5,000 every year. Check whether that works better for your present circumstance. You can generally raise your investment objectives later on. It's smarter to point a little lower – particularly at an early stage when you're attempting to make great contributing propensities – than to get debilitated out and out and surrender.

Altering Your Spreadsheet

If you as of now have a simple comprehension of Excel, when the down to earth tips that follow ought to be sufficient to manage you through how to change and refresh the spreadsheet.

Finding a workable pace Egg Amount

Your definitive objective in utilizing the investment spreadsheet is to connect numbers until you see the savings sum you landed at in Chapter 9 ("Calculate Your Nest Egg") show up in the Grand Total segment opposite the year wherein you in a perfect world wish to resign. Playing with the numbers and rates can assist you with making sense of how best to accomplish that objective.

If your procure enough to have the option to invest sizable measures of money every year, the procedure might be generally clear and you might be done in the blink of an eye. In any case, for all of us, it might take more time and exertion.

You may understand, for example, that you need to save significantly more than you suspected you did so as to arrive at your objective. By then you have some significant choices to make. You can either keep your aggressive yearly targets set up and focus on working considerably harder to accomplish them, or you can expand your time skyline (e.g., from 15 to 20 years) to give yourself more opportunity to arrive at your objective, or you can reevaluate your yearly salary needs in retirement and begin pondering how to resign on less.

All choices are on the table now. Try not to pay attention to everything as well: a lively and test frame of mind will help you in excess of a worried and baffled one. Try various methodologies like trying various caps and see which one fits you best. Resigning early is anything but a one-size-fits-all plan. Your answer should be custom fitted to accommodate your own conditions and needs.

What-If Scenarios

Since none of us can read the future, it bodes well to explore different avenues regarding diverse what if situations to perceive how they may influence you not far off. What if your investments just return 8% rather than 9%. Would you be able to at present arrive at your objectives? What if they return 11% or 12%. Why not test it out and see? What if your activity possibilities improve drastically and you begin contributing twofold what you figured you could part of the way through your investment years. Such was the situation for us. Why not run a what if situation that expect a multiplying of investment sums part of the way through your plan and perceive how it influences your outcomes.

Is My Goal Achievable?

When you've connected numbers that let you arrive at your objective in the time you'd like, when you need to ask yourself the immensely significant inquiry: Is this extremely reachable for me given my present circumstance? Will I truly save $10,000 one year from now?

Since at last your numbers must be grounded actually if this is to be something other than an activity in calculating. They need to jive with your certifiable conditions. So begin to consider where that $10,000 is truly going to originate from one year from now.

Maybe you have a 401(k) plan at work and you can consequently store 10% or a greater amount of your check easily into that. Also, maybe you can set up programmed payments from your financial indexes into a Roth IRA account every month. What amount can you truly save every month without driving things excessively far? Keep in mind, this is a long distance race, not a run, so you would prefer not to push so hard you make yourself or your family hopeless.

If you start to detect your favored situation, anyway wonderful in its result, is overambitious regarding its everyday requests on you or your family, have a go at easing off a piece. Lower your investment sums in the early years and perceive how that influences your general retirement plan.

Perhaps 15 years is essentially unreasonably aggressive for the present and you'll need to make due with 20 years – in any event until your material conditions improve. Keep in mind, whatever plan you land at, it's not unchangeable. You may hesitantly choose to focus on 20 years just to get a startling advancement at work, and out of nowhere 15 years is back on the table. That is an ideal opportunity to pull out your spreadsheet and have another look.

Let your real life direct the numbers you plug into your spreadsheet, particularly during the early years. Bind them to the real world. Attempt to envision truly saving the sum you see on paper in the coming year, and if you can do that and like it, when that is a genuine number that has genuine incentive to you and your circumstance.

If, then again, one year from now's number causes you to flinch, when it's back to the point where it all began. Attempt a more modest number until you can take a gander at it without feeling panicky. At last you need a number that doesn't make your palms sweat!

Getting Buy-In on Your Investment Plan

This is as acceptable a period as any to make reference to the significance of including your mate or huge other in the early retirement arranging process. It's dreadfully difficult to go only it with regards to putting something aside for early retirement – except if you happen to be well and genuinely single. If you're a couple, when you two ought to in a perfect world be in agreement.

Collaboration and Compromise

We urge you either to take a gander at the spreadsheet together and attempt various situations as a group – or else share the consequences of a few distinct situations with your companion and get info and purchase in from the get-go. Check whether the person in question is energetic about your general methodology. If you get the sense your plans are excessively forceful from their stance, see what you can do to mitigate them a piece.

Ideally your mate will be as energized as you are about resigning early, yet if not, you may need to think of a trade off plan. Make certain to tell your life partner how significant the possibility of early retirement is to you, yet in addition attempt to be adaptable about explicit retirement dates and yearly investment sums.

If your mate really wouldn't like to resign early as you do, that doesn't mean you fundamentally need to forsake your plans by and large. Truth be told it could make getting ready for retirement simpler rather than harder. If the individual in question really likes to keep working and isn't unduly put out at the idea of your resigning early, when you may need to save short of what you in any case would have. Your life partner will keep on accepting a pay, so a less thorough timetable of contributing might be required – which could be better answer for both of you.

Refreshing Your Spreadsheet with Actual Results

When your spreadsheet is set up, you should simply return to it once every year to survey how you're doing against plan. You'll connect genuine outcomes toward the finish of every year so you can anticipate future years utilizing genuine numbers rather than gauges. Every year you do this, the future turns into somewhat less fluffy on the grounds that you have all the more genuine information to work with. Likewise, the window until your objective retirement date keeps on narrowing, so there are less years in which you need to depend on instructed mystery to find a workable pace.

Keeping tabs on Your Development

Keeping tabs on your development lets you calibrate your plan en route and screen if you are still on course to resign by your deadline. We urge you to truly investigate your spreadsheet at any rate once per year so as to think about real performance against plan. Give some cautious consideration regarding how best to continue dependent on the undeniable realities before you.

What if You're Ahead of Schedule

Being in front of calendar is a fine issue to have: make the most of your favorable luck. If your material circumstance has improved – if you've gotten a significant raise at work, for instance – presently may be a decent time to consider raising your yearly investment sums for the years to come. By doing so you may find you can resign even sooner than anticipated, or else that you will have a bigger retirement fund than you suspected you would. Either prospect is very superb to consider.

What if You're Behind Schedule?

In case you're only a little off base at whatever year, there's no compelling reason to stress. That may basically be the after-effect of poor economic situations over the present moment, something over which you have essentially no control. If you're in a bear showcase, when it's not really amazing you aren't arriving at your normal objectives for the year. In any case, that is okay, you should let yourself know, since you're purchasing more portions of stock at a lower cost than you could have something else. In the positively trending business sector years that commonly trail a bear advertise, your profits are probably going to surpass desires, and in those years you ought to have the option to compensate for lost ground.

What if You're Way Off Track?

In case you're off track follow and have altogether less set aside than you figured you would before the finish of a specific year or series of years, when you have some genuine investment to do.

In the first place, attempt to decide why you missed the mark concerning your objectives. Did you invest as much as you had planned to? If not, maybe your objectives were basically excessively driven. You may need to bring them more into line with what you can really achieve and modify your all-inclusive strategy appropriately.

Then again, maybe the business sectors encountered an extreme downturn and through no flaw of your own you were brushed off kilter from where you figured you would be by this point. All things considered your yearly investment objectives aren't the issue, however you despite everything need to figure out how to refocus. It's horrible wishing things were better: you need to make them so. So choose which of the accompanying you need to do:

- Invest extra in the coming a very long time so as to get back up with your unique objectives.
- Increase your time skyline to give your investments more opportunity to compound and develop.
- Plan to manage with less in retirement, which means reexamining your spending and way of life decisions as you head into what's to come.

Obviously you can generally dare to dream the business sectors unequivocally outflank in the years to come and fix the issue for you. However, since that is totally beyond your ability to do anything about, it's risky to depend on – particularly in case you're altogether behind where you figured you would be. Better to bring matters into your own hands and modify your end-all strategy to realign it with your circumstance as it stands today. Else you chance falling further and advance behind on your objectives and feeling increasingly demoralized to where you basically choose to surrender – and that would be a genuine disgrace. Raise or lower your objectives to make them correspond with the real world, however don't surrender through and through or you'll be doing yourself an injury over the long haul.

Tracking Your Portfolio

You can follow your portfolio performance easily on your investment association's site, obviously, yet you may likewise need to make a basic portfolio tracker on Yahoo's Finance site page. You can pull it up immediately without entering a client name and secret phrase each time since there is no delicate data on the site. All it comprises of is the common store images and the quantity of offers you possess. Along these lines it offers a brisk method to check your aggregates and keep tabs on your development all the time.

To make your own portfolio tracker, go to Yahoo's Finance site, click on "My Portfolios," and select "Make Portfolio." Give your new portfolio a name (we call our own "Aggregate") and start adding common store images to it, trailed by the quantity of offers you possess for each. Hit save and you're ready. Simply click on "Include/Edit Holdings" if you need to change or refresh any data.

The main drawback to portfolio trackers like this is you need to occasionally refresh the offer data if you need to keep it current. The offer sums don't consequently refresh as they will without anyone else investment company's site.

Tracking Performance

We prescribe you save a duplicate of your investment spreadsheet every prior year rolling out any improvements to it. That way you have reinforcement if something ought to turn out badly. It additionally gives you a convenient authentic index if you ought to ever need to contrast your present spreadsheet with ones from earlier years.

Tracking Cumulative Goals versus Actuals

When you initially build up your yearly objectives, you might need to make an outline that lets you analyze combined objectives versus total actuals.

Your underlying plan speaks to a starting in particular, so don't anticipate accuracy of it past a year or two into what's to come.

Tracking Annual Investment Amounts

The last numbers you might need to follow are your yearly investment sums (objective versus genuine).

Chapter Twelve

Constantly Invest In Index Funds

When you have planned your investment spreadsheet, you should realize precisely the amount you have to invest over the coming year. Presently take that sum and gap by twelve to decide the specific sum you have to put every month so as to meet your yearly objective. All that remaining parts is to ensure you really invest that sum every month, paying little heed to how the market is performing.

There ought to be no doubt starting with one month then onto the next if you will invest: obviously you will invest. It doesn't make a difference what the business sectors are doing – regardless of whether they are up, down, or sideways. You have no power over that so you shouldn't worry about it. However, you do have authority over making your month to month investments as planned. Remain consistent with those month to month responsibilities and you'll have made your greatest stride towards accomplishing your objective of early retirement.

Put Your Investments on AutoPilot

The key to contributing routinely is to put your investments on autopilot. If you robotize the reserve funds process, it occurs without your pondering it – and that is something worth being thankful for, because you likely could be the cause all your own problems with regards to contributing on a customary calendar.

Things disrupt the general flow, costs include, money's tight, the business sectors are down, you're feeling disheartened, you would prefer not to write the check, you would prefer not to consider it at the present time, you don't have the opportunity or the vitality – the reasons the human personality can concoct not to accomplish something are downright stunning. Autopilot disposes of the greater part of those reasons.

Set It and Forget It

The best spot to begin computerizing your investments is grinding away. If your organization offers a 401(k) plan then you should pursue programmed findings from your check. Since the money is removed easily from your check before you ever observe it, it's as though it never existed in any case, so you don't miss it to such an extent. You don't need to leave behind it by hand – by composing a check, say, and seeing your checkbook balance get lower. Via computerizing the procedure, you've wiped out the core man – you – from the condition.

You can likewise set up programmed month to month moves easily out of your financial indexes into your assessable and Roth IRA accounts. You settle on the sum every month and which day of the month the exchange is made. It won't be very as imperceptible as the 401(k) process since you'll see the money vanish out of your financial indexes every month, except at any rate it's hands-off and you have less to consider, which is your objective. "Set it and overlook it" is a decent proverb with regards to contributing.

Mechanizing your investments keeps you on the directly to your yearly investment objective in a manner nothing else will. Your solitary obligation when becomes ensuring you have adequate assets close by to cover the programmed moves. Think about your month to month investments as you would your month to month contract payment. Doubtlessly you're going to make that payment: it is anything but an alternative, it's a need. That is the mentality you need to cultivate.

Pay Yourself First

You've presumably heard the articulation "pay yourself first," which means put resources into your own future first before covering different tabs or costs. That may sound somewhat outrageous; however it gives top need to you. Mechanizing your payments makes it undeniably more probable you won't avoid a payment to yourself. It pressures you to disclose more than what would have been prudent as it were, which isn't all awful when you consider what number of different things in life are getting out for you to burn through money on them. The alarm call of spending is somewhat simpler to oppose if you attach yourself to the pole like Odysseus and give yourself no other decision yet to keep with it.

So, make certain to leave yourself a little support when you select your month to month investment sum so you aren't pushing straight facing the deadline points of what you can deal with monetarily. Better to choose a littler sum you realize you can oversee throughout each and every month than to push excessively hard and end up stone cold broke at whatever month.

Consistency is your objective, not stretch and budgetary hardship. Leave your month to month contribution to your future alone a positive part of your life, something you can like, instead of a negative weight that puts a strain on your reality.

Use Dollar Cost Averaging

Putting your investments on autopilot lets you exploit a

strategy called dollar cost averaging. With dollar cost averaging you invest an equivalent measure of money every month in a profit paying little heed to the offer value, which implies you wind up obtaining more offers when costs are low and less offers when costs are high.

This methodology will in general lessen your normal offer cost after some time. A singular amount invested at the same time could be invested at simply an inappropriate minute when costs are particularly high. Dollar cost averaging protects you against advertise risk somewhat on the grounds that you spread your buys out equitably over an extensive stretch of time and over a scope of costs.

Suppose you choose to buy $100 every long stretch of a specific shared store for a quarter of a year. In the main month the store is valueed at $50, so your fixed month to month investment of $100 gets both of you shares. One month from now the valuation is $33 so your $100 gets you three offers. The most recent month it is $25 so your $100 gets you four offers. That is nine offers out and out which you've purchased at a normal cost of about $33 each ($300 ÷ 9). If you had put all $300 in a singular amount in the primary month, you would have paid $50 per share and just got six offers. By dollar cost averaging you have discounted your normal offer cost and decreased the market chance that can accompany contributing a single amount at the same time.

Dollar cost averaging likewise helps balance the regular human inclination to purchase a profit when it is performing admirably and not get it when it is performing ineffectively. We as a whole like a victor, isn't that right? Yet, purchasing an advantage when it is flying high methods getting it at a higher offer cost. Intelligently we should need to get it when it is failing to meet expectations and we can get more offers for our money, yet this isn't in every case how human instinct functions. Dollar cost averaging encourages us do what we ought to do in any case, which is purchase more portions of a investment when it is "on special" and less when it isn't.

What Others Say

My portfolio might be unreasonably traditionalist for you. Assuming this is the case, think about after an increasingly customary methodology:

- Safe portfolio—20 percent stocks, 80 percent bonds. For over 70 years, this portfolio has arrived at the midpoint of 7.0 percent a year. Its most noticeably awful year was lost 10.1 percent. It lost money 17 percent of the years.
- Balanced portfolio—50 percent stocks, 50 percent bonds. During a similar timespan, this portfolio has found the middle value of 8.7 percent a year. Its most exceedingly terrible year was lost 22.5 percent. It lost money 22 percent of the years.
- Risky portfolio—80 percent stocks, 20 percent bonds. This portfolio has found the middle value of 10.0 percent a year. Its most noticeably terrible year was lost 34.9 percent. It lost money 28 percent of the years.

You see the example, isn't that right? The more risky the portfolio, the more hearty the development was in the acceptable years. However, losses were more noteworthy during the terrible years and there were all the more awful years.

In picking which portfolio suits you best, think about your age. The more established you are, the fewer risks you should need to manage. Why? In case you're resigned, the reasonable outcomes of your losses can-not be soothed by your present place of employment salary. Regardless of whether you're not resigned, you basically do not have the advantage of having quite a few years to compensate for moderate-to-overwhelming losses.

A Closer Look at Stop-Losses:

The Exit Strategy That Professionals Use

One thing that professionals concur on is this: Whatever your methodology, will undoubtedly make some awful stock choices. Indeed, there's no assurance that your great choices will dwarf the terrible ones. Here's the uplifting news: It doesn't make a difference.

If you make twice the same number of terrible stock buy choices as great ones, shouldn't you lose twice as much as you've earned? No. Since stock contributing isn't just about purchasing. It's likewise about selling. As significant as purchasing the correct stocks at the ideal time is, it is similarly imperative to sell the correct stocks at the perfect time. And, you're not going to settle on indistinguishable selling choices for devaluing stocks from you would for acknowledging stocks.

Cut your loss. Ride your victors. Experts realize when to offer a stock and when to hold it by utilizing a trailing stop-loss.

The trailing stop expects you to follow the cost of your stock and sell it when it drops to a specific level. The sell point can be activated at 10 percent, 20 percent, 30 percent, or whatever, underneath the stock's most noteworthy selling cost. I prescribe 25 percent.

There's nothing magical about this number. It just appears to suit most stock leave circumstances. In any case, it carries one in number ramifications with respect to what your risk resistance ought to be. A decent proportion is one to three. That is, if you are happy to chance a 25 percent loss, you ought to sensibly expect in any event a 75 percent return on your investment. If you are told, for instance, that a 30 percent return however no higher is normal from a specific investment, your stop-loss point ought to be activated at 10 percent, not 25 percent.

Settle on an Overall Investment Mix

One of the most significant choices you can make as a financial specialist is choosing your general investment mix of stocks, bonds, and money. Your individual investments inside that mix are of auxiliary significance to the portfolio designation itself. Regardless of whether you purchase this specific stock or that specific stock is less significant than choosing the amount of your portfolio should comprise of stocks in any case.

Risk Tolerance and Time Horizon

Your investment mix ought to be your very own impression chance resilience and time skyline. Suppose you make some long memories skyline and a generally high resistance for chance (or if nothing else you figure you do; you'll know for sure after you've braved your first significant downturn). All things considered you might need to put vigorously in stocks and have only a foothold in bonds during your essential contributing years, since stocks offer the best potential for long haul development.

Then again, if you have a moderately low resilience for risk and suspect you won't have the option to rest around evening time if a lot of your money is riding on stocks, when you'll need to keep an increasingly adjusted plan of stocks, securities, and money to help cradle the instability that definitely accompanies owning just stocks.

Your time skyline to retirement is especially critical to consider while deciding your investment mix. A portfolio 80% to 100% put resources into the financial exchange may bode well in your start and core contributing years, yet as you close to retirement you have less time to recuperate from genuine downturns in the market. Surely once you resign you need a dependable source from which to pull back money if the financial exchange should crash, so having a strong situation in bonds gets vital. Capital protection and pay age become in any event as significant as the requirement for extra capital gratefulness once you resign.

During our essential contributing years we invested 100% (or extremely near it) in stocks and stock common assets. Our superseding objective during those years was capital appreciation. We weren't worried about market instability on the grounds that our time skyline was long enough by then that we realized we could brave whatever tempests may come. Indeed we saw downturns in the market as purchasing openings, and we profited by them once the business sectors ricocheted back and stock costs rose once more.

We stood by longer than was reasonable, however, to cut out a huge situation in bonds as we moved toward retirement. Truth be told it wasn't until we sold our home in the primary year of retirement and put the money into a security subsidize that we built up our first significant situation in quite a while. (Despite the fact that we had $30,000 set aside in a security support for use over the primary year of our retirement as an incomplete fence against risk.)

Fortunately for us things turned out, however looking back it would have been shrewder to gradually expand our bond possessions in the course of the most recent five years paving the way to retirement. When we could have distributed a portion of the money from the offer of our home to stocks and the rest to bonds dependent on our favoured investment mix as we entered retirement.

The Case for a More Conservative Approach

You may have seen from the table that you possibly need to forfeit a modest quantity of development if you have a portfolio comprising of 80% stocks and 20% bonds when contrasted with 100% stocks. The distinction in the normal yearly return is just 0.5% (9.9% versus 9.4%), which isn't a lot, particularly when you factor in the additional genuine feelings of serenity those bonds may give you. Indeed, even a 70/30 stock/bond portfolio offers an entirely decent normal yearly profit of 9.0% based for verifiable midpoints.

If you are a moderate, chance loath investor, you can breathe easy in light of this. It is as yet feasible for you to take a development planned position while moderating your risk somewhat by putting 70% in stocks and 30% in bonds. That would fulfil the requirement for capital thankfulness during your essential contributing years while as yet diminishing a portion of the instability en route.

One could seemingly do more awful than setting a 70/30 portfolio mix from the earliest starting point and keeping up that mix through life.

If you are put 70% or more in stocks, when you stand a decent possibility of arriving at your initial retirement objectives. Substantially less than that, in any case, and you start to get into a hazy area where you can in any case hope to arrive at your objective in the end, however maybe not as fast as you would have something else.

The Risk of Being Overly Conservative

Anything short of half stocks and half bonds/money during your essential contributing years and you start to enter what we would consider as an excessively traditionalist space where capital gratefulness takes a secondary lounge to the view of wellbeing. We state impression of security since it's a reasonable inquiry whether you truly are more secure with an excessively moderate portfolio mix. Why? Since there is more than one sort of risk with regards to contributing.

Amazingly moderate financial specialists will in general spotlight exclusively on advertise chance, which is the danger of losing money from variances in securities exchange costs (i.e., if stocks go down, you lose money). Many individuals are so scared of market risk they won't think about putting resources into stocks. They would prefer to place all their money in a financial balance gaining 1% premium. They accept they're avoiding any and all risks that way.

However, they're most likely not satisfactorily mindful of expansion risk, which is the risk swelling will consume their investments quicker than they can develop, bringing in their money worth less and less after some time. If expansion develops at 3% every year and their investments just gain 1%, when generally they are losing 2% every single year. Unexpectedly that sheltered financial balance doesn't appear to be so protected anything else, in any event with regards to their long haul purchasing power.

When individuals have a comprehension of expansion risk, they're commonly additionally ready to investigate a decent stock and bond portfolio. In spite of the real factors of market chance, the securities exchange by and large returns about 9% every year over the long haul and securities return all things considered about 5% to 6% every year. In this manner a well-adjusted stock and bond portfolio should keep you in front of expansion. You'll show signs of improvement genuine profit for your investment than you would with a "sheltered" ledger.

Keeping Fund Expenses Low

The normal shared store organization charges expenses multiple times higher than Vanguard's. These charges include after some time and have a critical effect to long haul performance.

Think about this: without any expenses by any means, a $100,000 portfolio gaining 9% every year would develop to $560,000 in 20 years. With a 1% yearly charge the last worth would be $458,000 – more than $100,000 less. If the yearly charge were 3%, which isn't impossible with some shared assets, the last worth would just reach $305,000 – more than $250,000 less. You can perceive any reason why charges matter and why we may choose to go with a investment firm like Vanguard therefore alone.

The topic of charges is considerably increasingly significant with regards to security reserves. A high expense can rapidly overpower a security store's presentation. For instance, if security finance returns 4% in a given year, when a 1% charge is equivalent to 25% of that arrival. If a similar store returns 1% in a given year, when a 1% charge successfully converts into a 0% return. In this manner a low-return condition, regardless of whether for stocks or bonds, just builds the significance of keeping charges low.

Vanguard's ultra-low costs apply to both stock and security reserves. To feature only two models, the cost proportions for its leader Index 500 Fund and its Total Bond Market Index Fund are an incredibly low 0.05% and 0.10% separately. (These are the cost proportions for the favoured Admiral Shares, which require a base reserve equalization of $10,000.) It's difficult to anticipate obviously superior to that.

Whichever investment firm you wind up picking, we suggest you ensure their costs are lower than the standard and that you keep your investments inside that solitary firm however much as could reasonably be expected for the good of simplicity. We additionally prescribe you look at the expenses charged as well as the scope of administrations offered by various investment firms before settling on a ultimate choice with respect to which one is directly for you. For example, if you want to do the vast majority of your putting resources into singular stocks as opposed to common assets, you may locate an online investment firm represent considerable authority in minimal effort stock exchanges that suits your needs superior to Vanguard.

Why Index Funds Make Sense

If you consider contributing basically an unfortunate obligation and not an enthusiasm all by itself, when file subsidize contributing may be the correct response for you. It's an extraordinary plan if you need to keep your budgetary life as easy and low-upkeep as could reasonably be expected.

With file subsidizes you quit attempting to beat the business sectors and rather just stay aware of them. File supports reflect the business sectors they track as opposed to attempting to beat them. They imitate as intently as conceivable the investment weighting and returns of the benchmark index they are intended to follow.

Maybe the most well known index store of all is likewise the first at any point made: the Vanguard 500 Index Fund, which tracks the S&P 500 Index. It was made by John Bogle of The Vanguard Group in 1975. Vanguard is currently the biggest shared reserve organization in the U.S., and the store has become a backbone of numerous an investment portfolio.

We like the reality index finances aren't helpless before any one individual, regardless of how good natured. Indeed, even a decent reserve administrator once in a while settles on terrible investment decisions. At that point, as well, dynamic reserve administrators once in a while resign or change investment firms or are supplanted, and the following chief may follow an impressively extraordinary and more hazardous investment procedure. You don't need to stress over this with an inactively overseen list subsidize. We think this makes file supports a progressively dependable investment over the long haul.

Tax Efficiency

Index supports will in general be very tax productive because offer turnover is negligible. Organizations are seldom added to or expelled from the S&P 500, for instance, so reserves following it once in a while need to purchase or sell shares. That implies there are less capital increases dispersions to stress over at charge time.

Index reserves are additionally easy to claim at charge season because the shared store organization gives all of you the data you have to provide details regarding your tax documents. Contrast this with an individual stock where you are liable for figuring and announcing the cost premise of the offers you have obtained, some of the time over a time of numerous years, when the offers are sold. Talking from individual experience, we can reveal to you this includes unwelcome confusions at charge time.

A Simpler Approach

With singular stocks it assists with having the option to read and comprehend an accounting report and a profit and misfortune explanation so as to effectively survey an organization's essential wellbeing. It requires some investment, exertion, and expertise to precisely evaluate a solitary organization and its stock, choose if the stock value speaks to a decent worth, and decide when to purchase the stock as well as when to sell it. Stock file assets by examination require less choices and less investigation.

Since they are comprised of hundreds (or here and there a huge number of) singular stocks, stock index reserves are purchase and-hold investments that by their very nature require little in the method for customized consideration. They must be evaluated in the total. You may assess the cost proportion of an Index 500 store, for instance, and choose whether or not the reserve is a solid match for your portfolio, yet it would look bad to dissect each of the 500 individual organizations making up the list since they are being sold as a bundle at any rate. You couldn't dismantle them regardless of whether you needed to.

By a similar token, security list subsidizes offer an a lot simpler way to deal with putting resources into bonds than experiencing the cerebral pains of laddering singular bonds. With a security subsidize you get proficient administration, wide enhancement, and high liquidity requiring little to no effort. There are no charges for purchasing or selling portions of no-heap security list finance, while the offer request that spread purchase and sell singular bonds can be very high. For convenience and ease, it's difficult to beat a decent security index subsidize.

With index assets all in all, your life doesn't need to rotate around your investments. You carry on with your life as typical and do the things you love to do. In the interim your investments are working for you out of sight without your giving a lot of consideration to them.

Not any more attempting to beat the business sectors. No all the more going through hours reading budgetary magazines and attempting to make sense of the following hot stock or the following hot shared reserve. Basically invest it, overlook it, and be finished. This purchase and-hold procedure makes your life (and your assessments) a lot less difficult. Rather than responding to the most recent market news, you protect yourself from those worries and spotlight on what you can control, which is your month to month contributions to the file finances you have picked.

Easy entry and Usability

A last advantage of common assets as a rule is that they offer superbly simple access with regards to purchasing and selling shares, moving offers among reserves, and pulling back money. This can be a significant factor when choosing where to invest your money.

Put resources into Your Core Holdings

Your core holdings are the bunch of investments that form the establishment of your portfolio. They are the investments you clutch for a lifetime. Hence you need to ensure they are top notch investments with a past filled with relentless performance.

We prescribe you utilize extensively expanded file assets as your core holdings. Only three stock file reserves are sufficient to give you overall inclusion for values. You truly needn't bother with more than that! To those you should include one more reserve for U.S. bonds. Here are the four store types we suggest for your core holdings:

1. S&P 500 Index Fund. A index support that mirrors the S&P 500 will give you expansive introduction to the main 500 enormous top organizations in the

U.S. Huge top represents huge capitalization, and these are the biggest, generally ground-breaking, and most well-promoted organizations in the U.S. Together they represent around three-fourths of the U.S. securities exchange's worth. Any reasonable person would agree no U.S.- based portfolio is finished without a S&P 500 index subsidize.

2. Broadened Market Index Fund. A file finance that mirrors the remainder of the U.S. financial exchange gives you expansive introduction to U.S. mid-top and little top stocks. Such assets commonly put resources into around 3,000 stocks representing around one-fourth of the market top of the U.S. financial exchange. An all-inclusive market store (or S&P culmination index) is viewed as a supplement to a S&P 500 list support, and together the two give presentation to the whole U.S. value showcase. Mid-and little top markets will in general be more unstable than the enormous top market yet in addition offer the potential for more significant yields as time goes on.

3. All out International Stock Index Fund. The world is greater than simply the U.S., so it bodes well to have presentation to the greatest, best, and quickest developing values from different nations around the world. Search for a index finance that gives you wide presentation to the all out global securities exchange, including both created and developing economies. Developing business sector stocks can be more unpredictable than local stocks, and money hazard can include significantly greater unpredictability. If

this is a worry for you, consider putting less right now the other two value reserves.

4. All out Bond Market Index Fund. A decent portfolio ought to incorporate a core store that mirrors the general U.S. investment grade security showcase. A complete security advertise reserve will normally invest around 33% of its profits in corporate securities and 66% in U.S. government obligations of shifting developments (short-, middle of the road, and long haul). While security finances will in general be delicate to increments in loan costs, their general dangers are lower than stock assets.

Any significant investment firm will offer file assets of these four kinds, so whichever firm you pick, you ought to have the option to discover great matches.

Rate to Invest in Each Fund

From the outset you may need to set aside enough to meet least store prerequisites for each reserve before proceeding onward to the following. In any case, when every one of the three assets are fully operational, you can invest as little as $100 every month naturally into each store starting now and into the foreseeable future. That makes it conceivable to put on a month to month premise in equivalent augmentations.

If you lean toward a more hazard opposed methodology, you might need to put a higher rate in the Index 500 store and a lower rate in the other two. Of the three assets, the International Stock reserve is most likely the most elevated hazard since it includes both money chance and developing business sector chance into the condition. Let your own inclinations direct you as far as the particular rates you decide to put resources into each sort of reserve: for instance, half Index 500, 30% Extended Market, 20% International Stock.

At the point when your monetary circumstance takes into consideration it, you ought to likewise make an underlying interest in a Total Bond Market list support. If you are designating basically 100% to stocks during the early and core long periods of your investment program, essentially keep the security support at the base level until further notice. At that point, around five years before your objective retirement date, start adding more to it.

If you like to keep up a 70/30 or 80/20 blend from the earliest starting point, at that point add to the security finance as a feature of your progressing investment assignment all through your essential contributing years. Remember whether you scale down your home once you resign, any additional value from the deal can make for a decent "flood" investment into your security support.

Abstain from Chasing Returns

It's enticing to go for large returns, particularly as a starting investor. You need to score huge and rake in some serious money, so once in a while, shockingly, your first investments end up being among your most noticeably terrible. Unquestionably that was the situation for us. Rather than purchasing basics file reserves, which appeared to be honestly exhausting to us at that point, we pursued the conceivably more significant yields offered by effectively oversaw and claim to fame reserves.

The Lure of Top 100 Lists

As amateur investors we scoured the money related magazines for the "most elite" common assets. Top 100 indexes that positioned assets dependent on their ongoing exhibition were a specific draw. Maybe it isn't too amazing hence that we ended up devotedly following the best assets on these rundowns and causing our underlying determinations from the ones to at or close to the top. Whatever store had played out the best in the course of the last five or ten years was the one we needed to put resources into next. Well-set promotions for the equivalent common finances would in general underscore the intelligence of putting resources into these assets over all others.

They state past performance is no assurance of future outcomes, and it turns out they would not joke about this. The issue with pursuing returns is that you wind up purchasing high and selling low – the specific inverse of what you need to do. Assets with outsized returns have frequently needed to face outsized challenges so as to get where they are at the highest point of the leaderboard. They once in a while remain there for long. The enormous wagers that got them there in any case regularly sink them once advertises move or financial specialist conclusion changes. Cost proportions can likewise be drastically higher for these high-flying assets, and that will in general force them back.

High Valuations, High Risks, High Expenses

If you need to purchase specialty advertise assets, at any rate hold back to do it until after you have a sound center portfolio developed. Area and claim to fame assets ought to be viewed as pastry, not the principle course.

Consistently purchasing minimal effort account assets may not be the most charming thing on the planet, yet wonder why you are putting resources into the primary spot. Is it for the surge that originates from making a major return? Or then again is it for the award of arriving at your retirement objective effectively? The race to score huge has more to do with betting than contributing, while a purchase and-hold way to deal with list support contributing is one you can use for an incredible duration as a solid system for getting rich gradually.

Different Options Besides Mutual Funds

Common supports aren't the main game around: there are other practical choices for getting rich gradually through a program of consistent investments. We'd prefer to contact quickly on a couple of these.

Exchange Traded Funds

Or ETFs, are close cousins of shared assets. They will in general be minimal effort and assessment proficient and they exchange like a stock. Though shared assets are purchased or sold toward the finish of each exchanging day, ETFs exchange for the duration of the day at costs that can be higher or lower than their net resource value. There is no base speculation prerequisite for ETFs – a key advantage to starting financial specialists – and you can invest to such an extent or as little money as you wish.

ETFs likewise offer tax breaks to financial specialists. Common finances must disperse capital increases to their investors on a yearly premise (i.e., at whatever point shares have been sold at a profit so as to keep the portfolio in accordance with the weighted account being followed). These additions are assessable regardless of whether you reinvest the dispersions in more portions of a similar store. By correlation, financial specialists in ETFs for the most part possibly acknowledge capital increases when they sell shares. This gives them more command over when they understand capital gains and need to pay charges on them.

Most ETFs track a account and are in this manner exceptionally differentiated. They can hold stocks, bonds, and even wares. Their cost proportions will in general be lower than those for practically identical common assets. One purpose behind this is an ETF doesn't need to keep up a money save for recoveries. The Vanguard S&P 500 ETF (VOO), for instance, has a ultra-low 0.05% cost proportion. That matches the cost proportion for the "Chief naval officer Shares" variant of its Index 500 store and is lower than the "Financial specialist Shares" rendition.

Financier commissions here and there apply when you are purchasing or selling an ETF. A significant exemption is ordinarily made, in any case, when you are purchasing or selling ETFs offered by your own investment firm. For instance, Vanguard ETFs can be purchased and sold sans commission through Vanguard Brokerage Services. To dishearten day exchanging, Vanguard permits 25 free exchanges of a similar ETF in a year time span before confining further exchanging for 60 days.

An enhanced ETF list finance held over the long haul can be a strong investment decision, however the very capacity of an ETF to exchange like a stock can now and then be a drawback in that it builds the compulsion to take part in showcase timing or momentary hypothesis.

In any case, there is a great deal to like about ETFs and very little to disdain. We can positively observe the ethics of putting resources into them. Maybe out of a feeling of nature if nothing else, we have stayed committed common reserve speculators. We accept shared assets and ETFs offer generally practically identical encounters as long as you are as of now contributing with a minimal effort speculation firm like Vanguard.

Singular Value Stocks

Singular stocks offer another commendable option in contrast to common assets or ETFs. If you choose to go this course, make certain to give yourself fundamental training in money related issues first so you have the basis should have been an insightful financial specialist. We suggest you read a book or two about Warren Buffett, broadly thought about the best speculator of the twentieth century, to get a thought of his worth way to deal with contributing.

Buffett's recommendation at its most essential is to buy organizations at a huge markdown to their characteristic worth, which means staying away from high-flying development stocks and adhering rather to organizations that are underestimated by the market for some explanation. These organizations might be incidentally on the ropes however are probably going to make a solid rebound.

If you can figure out how to be a contrarian financial specialist and purchase stocks when they're whipped however on a very basic level sound, you'll have gone far towards turning into a savvy speculator. It's anything but difficult to be attracted by tech organizations making hot items, however these equivalent stocks are as often as possible overrated in light of the fact that such a large number of others need them as well, and typically for an inappropriate reasons. By examination, what may resemble an exhausting old worth stock from the outset can sneak up all of a sudden. Rather than concentrating on what an organization does, we prescribe you focus on what it returns. Leave that alone the deciding element in whether you regard an organization to be energizing or not.

Bear markets can be a keen financial specialist's closest

companion. Look out for stocks that have been battered alongside the market all in all despite the fact that their basics are sound. You can likewise search for organizations that have been thumped in the news as of late yet are naturally stable. Netflix rings a bell as an ongoing model. A progression of administrative stumbles sent the stock forcefully descending, yet the basic plan of action was sound and the organization kept on winning profits. A shrewd speculator may have stepped in and bought shares when they were at or close to their lows and received the profits later on.

In some cases an open door tags along that isn't accessible to the overall population.

The significant drawback to putting resources into singular stocks is that your hazard is higher on the grounds that you're put resources into just a bunch of stocks one after another. You're significantly less expanded than you would be with a file finance, and if a couple of your stocks should dive, it could bigly affect your portfolio. Then again, in case you're a canny financial specialist and your stocks perform well, you remain to profit in a major way.

Sadly the vast majority of us aren't as sharp at stock picking as Warren Buffett, so except if you are especially sure of your capacities right now, would prescribe you stick to file finance contributing as the more secure and increasingly dependable methodology. A mix of list support contributing and value stock contributing is likewise worth considering.

Some other Options?

We'll quickly make reference to two different choices that ring a bell for arriving at your initial retirement objectives.

Purchasing and selling land offers a doable way to deal with accomplishing money related autonomy, if you have a decent comprehension of your nearby land advertise and a sharp eye for value. Now and again this may include flipping homes, where you put sweat value into a fixer-upper at that point exchange it at a profit, and in others it may include setting up an assortment of investment properties in your neighbourhood you oversee and lease on a month to month premise. We don't dare to offer guidance regarding this matter since it was not the methodology we took. We only notice it since we are aware of other people who have taken this attach to making a month to month pay stream and it worked for them. We presume it would request more active exertion, however, and might expect you to be genuinely present to deal with the business after you resigned.

Another alternative worth referencing is turning into a business person and going into business. Obviously anything is possible with this methodology: you couldn't possibly get rich gradually yet make easy money if you hit upon the correct business opportunity. Then again, the danger of being a business person can be very high so it takes boldness to pick this choice. In actuality all your investments are tied up on one place – your business – so if it bombs your fantasy of early retirement can flop alongside it, or if nothing else be derailed a period. In any case, if it succeeds it could offer generous monetary prosperity and a real feeling of achievement.

For the individuals who have the creativity and personality for it, the innovative way can be a fantastic and remunerating one. For all of us, a solid activity and some straightforward list finance contributing might be the best course. Unwavering mindsets always win in the end for the greater part of us and offers what might be the most secure way to early retirement.

Chapter Thirteen

Set Up Your Pension Plan

Welcome to the great universe of extraordinary retirement bargains for entrepreneurs and independently employed people. Your business—regardless of whether it's full-or low maintenance, with or without peed your way to an effortless retirement. At the point when you work for yourself, you in a flash fit the bill to structure your own expense supported retirement plan in which you make major decisions. The reason is this: Because you are independently employed or work a private company, you have no annuity plan from any semblance of an IBM, AT&T or General Motors to cover your retirement needs.

Regardless of how little your business—regardless of whether only you make up the whole staff—it has similar fundamental rights the mammoths need to introduce and support an appealing profits plan for you and workers. For instance, you can:

- Choose from a trio of plans that let you put aside as much as 25% of income—or $40,000, whichever is less—every year. Each dollar that you invest is charge deductible.

- Write your own retirement ticket with an plan that lets you set an individual retirement-pay target, at that point set aside—and deduct—whatever is important to meet it.

- Select a "business IRA" with basic administrative work and a contribution limit that goes as high as $30,000, com-pared with the customary IRA's $3,000 (in 2002 and ascending to $5,000 by 2008) roof.

- Use a "straightforward" plan to put aside up to $7,000 (for 2002) of your profit for your retirement, regardless of whether that is 100% of your business pay. On account of the Economic Growth and Tax Relief Reconciliation Act of 2001, the yearly sum you may put aside ascends to $10,000 by 2005. If you are age 50 or older you can make extra make up for lost time contributions to your SIMPLE plan— $500 in 2002 ascending to an extra contribution of $2,500 in 2006.

There's additional. While most annuity plans necessitate that you put in a safe spot a similar rate for your workers that you accomplish for yourself, a contort lets some entrepreneurs tip their plans in their own kindness if their representatives are more youthful than they are.

Right now, mention to you what you have to think about every one of these plans so as to pick the best fit for your conditions.

Profits plan rudiments are amazingly comparative whether you're Microsoft or Jane Entrepreneur producing $5,000 of independent work salary from a business in your carport.

With a "defined contribution" retirement plan, your business (even a one-individual business) can put aside a level of income every year. A "defined advantage" plan works backward. As in the TV game show Jeopardy!, you start with the appropriate response—a yearly retirement-salary focus based on your personal preference—at that point give the inquiry. What amount must I invest yearly to arrive at that objective? This plan lets you set aside whatever sum is important to meet your in-come target.

Similarly as with organization gave plans and IRAs, the tax reductions offered by plans for private companies and the independently employed accompany a catch: Because this should be retirement investment funds, you need to make a deal to avoid dunking into the money early. There's a 10% corrective ty (potentially 25% for SIMPLE IRAs) if you tap the air conditioner check too early, and most definitely that is for the most part whenever before you arrive at age 591/2 or, if you leave or close the business that is producing the salary, age 55.

The Keogh Plan: A Sweet Deal

He fundamental retirement program for independently employed people is regularly called a Keogh plan, named after Donald Keogh, the congressman whose enactment approved the tax reductions that make the plan work. A false name for Keogh is the H.R. 10 plan, a reference to the enactment itself. Some plan supports don't utilize either name, however, and rather allude to the plan basically as either a defined contribution plan or a defined advantage plan.

By whatever name you call it, this is a sweet plan. Contributions are completely charge deductible, and the plan fills in as an expense cover—there's no assessment on income until you pull back the money, apparently in retirement. This gives the Keogh the equivalent supercharged procuring limit as an IRA.

Who Qualifies?

You meet all requirements for a Keogh plan if you gain any independent work salary:

- as proprietor or sole owner in a full-time or low

maintenance independent investment, regardless of whether consolidated or unincorporated;

- as part proprietor in a business association;
- as an independently employed proficient;
- from a sideline or "working two jobs" business you work from your home or somewhere else; or
- as an independently employed free-lancer, speaker, teacher or expert.

For whatever length of time that you have pay from any of these sources, you can set up a Keogh, regardless of whether you likewise make some full-memories work and take an interest in your boss' retirement plan at work.

How a Plan Might Work

State that you're an independently employed 40-year-old making

$52,000 every year and figure that your salary will rise a normal of 5% yearly. You set up your own profits plan and reserve 13% of your income (all assessment deductible) into the account every year. This is what occurs if the money wins a normal return of 10% every year:

- In ten years: You'll have invested a completely charge deductible $85,000 in your retirement account and it will be worth about $144,000.
- In 15 years: Your deductible contributions complete $146,000 and the estimation of your retirement fund has hit $313,000.
- In 20 years: You've presently invested, and discounted,

$224,000. However, your retirement fund has zoomed to $608,000.

- In 25 years: Retirement shows up, and the $323,000 you've added to your profit sharing retirement plan has developed to $1 million.

Saving similar sums outside the Keogh—exposed to the harsh elements, unfeeling reality where after-charge dollars are invested and the expense man asserts a portion of every year's profit—would desert you far. Make that FAR behind. Since you're setting aside after-charge money, there's less to put aside every year, and the yearly expense bill restrains development of your retirement fund:

- In ten years: Since charges are paid on the 13% of your profit before the money is saved, you have invested just about $60,000, and the estimation of the account (with charges paid every year on the income) will be about $86,000.

- In 15 years: You've invested $102,000 and your retirement fund is $173,000.

- In 20 years: The estimation of your assessable retirement fund is about $309,000—around half as much as the $608,000 in the Keogh.

- In 25 years: Things aren't beating that. The estimation of nondeductible investments is about $518,000, com-pared with the $1 million in the Keogh.

Indeed, the Keogh money is burdened when you take it.

However, you'll despite everything be grinning.

Or on the other hand consider a 44-year-old independently

employed couple going for a $1-million savings and retirement at age 62. Their consolidated pay of $85,000 is additionally rising 5% every year, except they decide on an alternate sort of profits plan that fixes their yearly put aside at 20% of their independent work income every year—up to a most extreme $40,000 every year each. They take assessment reasoning for everything. If the money acquires a normal return of 10% inside the plan, here are the outcomes:

- In five years: The couple's $94,000 in contributions has developed to $125,000.
- In ten years: The retirement fund hits $361,000.
- In 15 years: The retirement pot has expanded to $777,000.
- In 18 years: The couple has put $451,000 in charge deductible dollars and at age 62 has more than $1 million in their account.

The Blessings of a Keogh

As noted above, contributions to your own annuity plan are in every case completely charge deductible, regardless of how high your pay and whether or not you or your life partner is secured by another retirement plan. There's nothing of the sort as a nondeductible contribution, as there is with an IRA. And, you can have an IRA—conventional or Roth—notwithstanding your Keogh. (Regardless of whether customary IRA contributions would be deductible relies upon your pay, in light of the fact that the Keogh is viewed as a business gave plan to reasons for the IRA deductibility tests.)

What amount would you be able to invest? That relies upon how a lot of independent work salary you have and what sort of Keogh you pick. The deadline points by and large range from 15%

to 25% of your independent work income, to a limit of $30,000 to $40,000 every year.

The significant disadvantage to having your own private company profits plan is this: If you have workers, they should be remembered for the plan and you should essentially invest indistinguishable level of pay to their accounts from you add to your own. There's a significant special case to that standard, called an age-weighted plan, examined later right now.

PROFIT SHARING PLANS FOR MAXIMUM FLEXIBILITY

You can put as much as 15% of your net independent work income, up to a limit of $30,000, into a profit sharing defined contribution plan. Calculating those incomes gets somewhat precarious, without a doubt. Business profit for an independently employed individual methods your net business pay less the sum you con-tribute to your Keogh, less one-portion of any standardized savings charge you pay on your independently employed income. If you have another activity where government disability is deducted and you acquire over the yearly standardized savings greatest, there won't be any extra government managed savings charge on your independent work pay. Something else, this counterbalance has the impact of somewhat decreasing your Keogh contribution.

To slice through the math, and to keep things straightforward, we've utilized 13% of pay as the appropriate cover on profit sharing Keogh contributions. That is 13% of net independent work profit, disregarding the Keogh contribution itself and the government managed savings charge balance.

The key bit of leeway to a profit sharing plan is adaptability.

You don't need to contribute a similar level of income consistently—you can place in 13% one year, 6% one more year, even skirt a year if your accounts totally compel you to curtail. If you are unsure about your capacity to add to the plan every year or then again if you would prefer not to secure yourself in a set rate contribution, this is your best decision.

State, for instance, you have your own photography studio however your pay is exceptionally inconsistent. A few years you feel flush—a lot of additional batter to store for retirement. Different years you're unable to make the home loan. A profit sharing plan lets you move with the independent work punches, placing in more money in great years and less money in terrible ones. As an end-result of that adaptability, the sum you are permitted to con-tribute is lower than in different plans.

Money PURCHASE PLANS FOR HIGHER LIMITS.

In money buy defined contribution plan, you can contribute up to 25% of your net independent work income. Once more, net is defined as the sum that is left after you subtract your contribution. To take an easy route through the math, utilize 20% of independent work profit. The government managed savings charge balance may bring down this a piece. The top yearly contribution right now.

The large in addition to with a money buy plan is that you can take care of more money toward your effortless retirement. This is a breathtaking decision if you meet three criteria: you have independent work salary over other business compensation, you can stand to dedicate a huge part of the independent work pay to retirement investment funds and you hope to have the option to keep subsidizing your plan at a similar level a seemingly endless amount of time after year.

A downside of money buy plans is that once you choose what level of pay you need to contribute, you should contribute that rate every year regardless of how high or low your independent work salary. If you choose for make a 20% contribution, state, you're required to contribute 20% every year. Essentially, you exchange the adaptability of profit sharing for the capacity to contribute a more prominent sum.

Money buy plans will work best for you if you have a genuinely relentless, unsurprising salary from your independent investment or other independent work.

HAVE IT BOTH WAYS.

An eminent procedure to catch both the adaptability of a profit sharing plan and the higher furthest reaches of a money buy annuity is to have the two kinds of plans. That is consummately legitimate, and it's a simple method to remove the ideal retirement fund building potential from your independent work pay. Here's the means by which to tap the most extreme duty deductible advantage for your plan:

To begin with, set up a money buy design and submit a fixed 7% of your independent work income to this annuity consistently. That is currently your base yearly profits financing contribution, yet at that unobtrusive level it shouldn't be too difficult to even consider meeting.

At that point, set up a profit sharing plan that can be independently financed for up to 13% a greater amount of your independent work pay. For whatever length of time that your contributions to the two plans together complete close to 20% of your profit (up to the $40,000 yearly top), you're inside the built up limits. You have the adaptability to modify your contribution year to year yet in addition the capacity to place in as much as the law permits, if you can bear the cost of it.

This methodology has another bit of leeway in that it forces some order on you, expecting you to set aside at any rate 7% of your salary yearly. However, it additionally permits you to about triple your contribution, to a most extreme 20%. Regardless of whether you can't bear the cost of that high a contribution now, incorporating as far as possible with your program while restricting your pledge to 7% of profit is an incredible method to give yourself space to develop and quicken your retirement plan later on.

The Age-Weighted Plan Opportunity

The "age weighted" or age-based profit sharing annuity plan works a lot of like a Keogh plan, however if you have representatives and the age differential among you and them is enormous, this could be a super plan for building your retirement savings. This plan is particularly appropriate to entrepreneurs in their fifties whose representatives are more youthful by a normal of around ten years or more. You despite everything need to remember workers for the plan. However, you can quicken your own retirement reserve funds while taking care of less for your workers.

To see the potential, consider a 55-year-old entrepreneur whose three workers are 45, 35 and 25 years of age. Under a standard profit sharing plan, if the proprietor contributes 13% of salary (rising to about 15% of overall gain after the contribution is made) to her own plan, she should likewise set aside 15% of the net income for her three representatives. State the proprietor's net gain is $75,000 and her workers' are $30,000, $25,000 and $20,000, separately. At 15% of net in-come, the proprietor's yearly annuity contribution would be about $11,250 and the workers would get $11,250 isolated among them three (15% of their consolidated total compensation of $75,000).

The age-weighted equation drastically changes all that and permits the proprietor to put undeniably a greater amount of the complete retirement-money contribution ($22,500 right now) her own account. Utilizing a table that appoints a particular markdown factor to every individual dependent on age and years to retirement, this 55-year-old entrepreneur can help her own contribution to $17,780, while diminishing representative contributions to an aggregate of $4,720. If you figure this sort of plan may function admirably for you, connect with a bookkeeper or monetary organizer who has involvement with retirement arranging.

The Simplicity of a Business IRA

There is an option in contrast to the Keogh, a super-ease, low-support plan: the "business IRA," which allows completely charge deductible contributions far over the $3,000 as far as possible for singular IRAs.

This plan, called a streamlined worker annuity (SEP), or SEP-IRA, is simpler to set up and requires less continuous administrative work than a Keogh or other independent investment profits plan. Much the same as the perplexing annuity programs offered by enormous organizations, SEPs convey significant duty reserve funds to both you and your workers. Your business or independent work assessable pay is decreased by the measure of money you put into the SEP. Furthermore, the money in your plan, remembering income for speculations, becomes untaxed until you pull back it. Pretty much anybody with pay from independent work—sole owners, accomplices, proprietors of partnerships or S companies, even specialists and moonlighters—is qualified to open a SEP. Regardless of whether you procure a couple of bucks selling creates on ends of the week or you're an establishing accomplice in a powerful counselling firm, you fit the bill for a SEP.

A SEP is a cross between a profit sharing Keogh plan and a conventional IRA. Your contributions go into an exceptional SEP-IRA. You can contribute as much as 15% of your net independent work profit, up to a maxi-mum of $30,000. Once more, net methods the sum that is left after you subtract your contribution and the counterbalance for any government managed savings charges paid on independent work pay. For the wellbeing of simplicity, figure 13% of net in-come—not including those two components—is the point of confinement.

You are allowed to fluctuate your contributions every year or even skirt a year, as conditions warrant. If you have qualified workers, you should add to their SEP-IRAs every year you add to your own.

There's only one structure for the business to round out to open a SEP, and all the money you contribute for yourself and your workers is deductible as a cost of doing business. Representatives—not you—pick how their money is contributed, so you're calmed of that stress.

Another bit of leeway: You can open and reserve a SEP up until your expense accounting deadline time—for the most part April 15—including any expansions.

The SIMPLE Plan for Small Business

This tax reduction is one more plan intended to en-mental fortitude self-employeds to put something aside for retirement.

Straightforward means "investment funds motivating force coordinate designs for representatives." These plans were truly made by Congress as a rearranged retirement plan for little organizations—just firms with less than 100 workers can utilize a SIMPLE, and if you have workers, you should remember them for your plan. In any case, the entryway to SIMPLEs is additionally open to independently employed labourers without any representatives. Regardless of whether your business is full-time or you do independent or counselling work notwithstanding an all day work, you can have a SIMPLE. And, you can have one regardless of whether you have an occupation that offers an annuity plan. You may not, in any case, have both a SIMPLE and a Keogh.

There are really two sorts of SIMPLE plans—a SIMPLE IRA and a SIMPLE 401(k). All things considered, the IRA variant will be best for an independently employed individual without any representatives, so is what's examined here.

The profit of a SIMPLE IRA is that you can stash up to $7,000 every year (for 2002) a year into the plan—regardless of whether that is 100% of your independent work in-come. With the 20%-of-pay top that applies to Keogh plans, you need overall gain from your business of in any event $35,000 to make a $7,000 contribution. Utilizing the SEP, you'd need $53,681 in independent work pay to contribute $7,000. So if your business in-come is under those levels—and you can stand to put aside $7,000 per year for your retirement—a SIMPLE is particularly charming. (All things considered, the SIMPLE can be a champ regardless of whether your business pay is higher in light of the fact that you might have the option to help the sum added to the plan with a business "coordinate" to the plan. The match can be 2% or 3% of your salary.)

Contributions to a SIMPLE IRA can be deducted on your arrival, and profit inside the account is charge conceded. Similarly as with conventional IRAs, there's typically a 10% punishment if you pull back assets before age 59 1/2—yet the punishment is an astounding 25% if you haul money out before 59 1/2 and you've been in the plan for under two years.

You have until the documenting deadline time for your assessment re-go to make your SIMPLE contribution for the earlier year, yet there is a trick: The plan probably has been opened by October 1 of the year for which the contribution is being made. As with Keoghs, SEPs and IRAs, SIMPLEs are offered by banks, financier firms and shared assets.

Write Your Own Retirement-Pay Ticket

Regularly, an entrepreneur sets up a profits plan when the business is steady and gainful enough to manage the cost of it. At that point, you might be in your mid forties to fifty or more established, and the $40,000 or 20% breaking points in different plans may not be sufficient to connect the retirement-salary hole that weaving machines.

All things considered, you have another choice: the defined advantage plan. It lets you flip-flop your methodology. You choose how much pay you need to get in retirement and the law lets you put aside enough current salary to arrive at that objective—and deduct each dime. This kind of plan can be alluring if:

- You need to manufacture major retirement finance as quick as would be prudent. This likely methods you've procrastinated on your plan and are presently playing make up for lost time;

- You are inside 15 years or so of your focused on retirement date;

- You can stand to sink a major piece of your yearly in-come into the plan. That implies you are prosperous and have a genuinely unsurprising salary; and

- You have no workers.

The significant downsides to defined advantage plans are their cost and Rube Goldberg–like multifaceted nature. Each plan is special; contingent upon your age, future and monetary conditions, and will include some confused math. You'll require a legal advisor, bookkeeper, statistician or other money related expert to assist you with setting everything up and make sense of the necessary yearly commitment every year. The IRS is severe about adhering to the principles on computing commitments to abstain from overfunding your plan.

A 50-year-old acquiring $80,000 who needs to resign at 62 and get a profits of $4,500 every month would at first contribute about $25,000 every year to the plan, expecting the money will develop at a 8% yearly rate, as indicated by Sam Gilbert, leader of the annuity counselling firm United Plan Administrators, in Westlake Village, Cal. All in all, the more established you are, the more you'll have to place into the plan, in light of the fact that the money has less time to develop individually. The commitment is balanced yearly and could rise generously in future years.

That makes defined advantage plans a profoundly requesting decision. You should think of enough yearly financing to in the end arrive at the pay level you've chosen. If you neglect to meet your objectives, the plan could be punished or broke up. And, if you have representatives close to your own age who might likewise fit the bill for profits inclusion, a similar math that converts into robust annuity commitments for you converts into powerful profits commitments for them, as well.

The Right Plan for You

Settling on the correct decision among do-it-without anyone's help annuity plans will rely upon the kind of business you work, your age, how a lot of money you can bear to save, and whether you have representatives. These situations can enable you to pick what's best for you:

- Employee with a sideline business or working two jobs; independent work pay under $25,000. The SIM-PLE IRA permits you to store $7,000 of your independent work pay every year—that is 28% of $25,000, a bigger offer than a SEP or Keogh plan would acknowledge.

- Self-utilized specialist; no workers; dubious salary. If you work for yourself and independent from anyone else, and are genuinely sure you'll never go over the 13% ($30,000 top level augmentation) limit on a profit sharing plan, an essential SEP is the most ideal approach. You get the tax breaks, keep the privilege to change your commitments year to year and have the least difficult desk work conceivable.

- Self-utilized proficient; no workers; high, stable salary. A money buy Keogh plan is your pass to boosting yearly commitments to 20% ($40,000 most extreme). If it's all the same to you some additional desk work, twin plans—a profit sharing and a money buy—get you the 20% cover alongside adaptability to shift commitments. In case you're as of now in your fifties and have minimal saved for retirement, a defined advantage Keogh might be your best decision for quickly fabricating your savings.

- Self-utilized proficient with barely any representatives. An age-weighted profit sharing plan might be the most ideal approach if your workers are more youthful than you by a normal of around ten years or more. Your commitments can vary year to year and you can save more for yourself than for your more youthful workers.

- Owner of a little eatery with for the most part low-paid, high-turnover representatives. A SEP is a decent decision here. The stunt? Structure the plan so just workers who have been with your business for three of the first five years are qualified to take an interest. That lets you amplify commitments for yourself and limit the expense of commitments for workers.

- Owner of a little retail location with numerous regular yet long-lasting representatives. A SEP will presumably not be a decent decision if you utilize countless low maintenance or occasional laborers. SEP rules state you should likewise add to their retirement plans, regardless of whether they make as little as $400 or so in a year. A profit sharing Keogh is a superior decision since representatives must work for you at any rate 1,000 hours in a year to fit the bill for incorporation in the plan.

www.ingramcontent.com/pod-product-compliance
Lightning Source LLC
Chambersburg PA
CBHW052357220526
45465CB00003BB/1145